Reducing Crime, Reducing Incarceration

Essays on Criminal Justice Innovation

Reducing Crime, Reducing Incarceration

Essays on Criminal Justice Innovation

Greg Berman

CONTEMPORARY SOCIETY SERIES

Quid Pro Books

New Orleans, Louisiana

Published in 2014 by Quid Pro Books.

ISBN 978-1-61027-211-7 (pbk.)
ISBN 978-1-61027-212-4 (eBook)

QUID PRO BOOKS

5860 Citrus Blvd., Suite D-101
New Orleans, Louisiana 70123
www.quidprobooks.com

qp

Publisher's Cataloging-in-Publication

Berman, Greg.
   Reducing crime, reducing incarceration : essays on criminal justice innovation / Greg Berman.
      p. cm. — (Contemporary society)
   Includes index and bibliographical references.
   ISBN 978-1-61027-211-7 (paperback edition)
1. Criminal justice, Administration of—United States. 2. Courts—United States. 3. Crime prevention—United States. 4. Judges—Judicial Process. I. Title. II. Series.
HV7343.B86 2014   377.543'6—dc22
                                                                       2014045537

Author photograph © Rick Kopstein/*New York Law Journal*, used by permission.
Cover design © 2014, dammsavage studio.
Interior design © Michele Veade.

Contents

For my mom and my dad

FOREWORD

Looking back over four decades of involvement in criminal justice policy—through two stints as Assistant Attorney General in the Clinton and Obama Administrations and now as a professor of criminology, law and society at George Mason University—it's clear to me that things have changed for the better in our field.

When I was first working at the American Bar Association in the 1970s, criminal justice was largely dominated by bad news—research that suggested "nothing works" in rehabilitating offenders, a steady stream of media coverage about urban violence, and high levels of public fear of crime. The federal government's role in backing research and criminal justice innovation was still being defined, just a few years after the Johnson Crime Commission had called for federal support to states and localities in addressing crime.

Since that time, tremendous progress has occurred. I've been particularly heartened by the way practitioners and policymakers at all levels of government rely more today on evidence and data—and less on ideology and anecdote—in their decision-making about programs, strategies and resource allocation. This shift can also be measured in public attitudes: As mayors and other municipal leaders adopt "smart on crime" strategies to make streets safe, citizens are recognizing that crime and disorder are not inevitable components of urban life.

Reducing Crime, Reducing Incarceration vividly documents this movement within criminal justice. It describes a set of criminal justice reforms that seek to engage with the public in new ways, to make greater use of alternatives to incarceration, and to use data to measure impact. These new ideas include community courts, drug courts, mental health courts, and other examples of problem-solving justice.

These initiatives—along with similar ones like HOPE probation and problem-oriented policing—exemplify American innovation. They tap the entrepreneurial energy of creative thinkers to advance core values of the American justice system: protecting both individual rights and the safety of our communities. While we still have a lot to learn, the U.S. Department of Justice's "what works" clearinghouse (*www.crimesolutions.gov*) highlights dozens of programs that have been shown to improve public safety and reduce the use of jail and prison.

It would be hard for me to think of anyone better positioned to tell this story of criminal justice reform than Greg Berman. As the director of the Center for Court Innovation, Greg has been an active participant in the fight to make our justice system more fair and more effective. Since I first met him nearly twenty years ago, I have been impressed over and over again by his creativity and his vision.

When I was first working with the Center in the 1990s, its sole focus was the Midtown Community Court in Manhattan. What I loved then and continue to love today about the agency is its commitment not just to testing new ideas but to documenting results, as well. They knew what they were doing was untried and unproven. And they knew that if they couldn't show results and impact, their model would never be anything more than a neat idea.

With the benefit of hindsight, we know that the Center for Court Innovation turned the Midtown Community Court into a success. We also know that this team of researchers and planners went on to launch numerous other successful experiments, some of which are highlighted in this book.

It isn't easy to innovate within the criminal justice system. The obstacles are enormous: heavy caseloads, rigid bureaucracies, outmoded facilities, shrinking budgets, and internal resistance to new ideas. The Center for Court Innovation is one of the very few organizations I know that has been consistently able to overcome these impediments to create meaningful change again and again.

Reducing Crime, Reducing Incarceration is honest about cataloging these challenges. One of the things I like about this book is its modesty—and its insistence that, over time, even seemingly modest improvements can produce significant change. The spirit of the book is ultimately one of pragmatic optimism.

In *Reducing Crime, Reducing Incarceration,* Greg Berman offers vivid testimony that—even in the face of opposition—it is, in fact, possible to push our criminal justice system closer to realizing its highest ideals. And that, indeed, is good news.

LAURIE ROBINSON
Clarence J. Robinson Professor of
Criminology, Law and Society,
George Mason University

October 2013

Reducing Crime, Reducing Incarceration

Essays on Criminal Justice Innovation

INTRODUCTION

A few years ago, I stumbled across the work of sociologist Peter Rossi and his oft-quoted Iron Law of Evaluation: "The expected value of any net impact assessment of any large-scale social program is zero."

It seems strange to say, but I was immediately drawn to Rossi's law. Indeed, I found his cautionary note motivating. Rossi reminds us that solving social problems is difficult work that does not lend itself to simple solutions or short turnarounds. An instinctive moderate, I am attracted to the idea that there are no silver bullets or short cuts to social change—just a series of small, methodical steps over a long time horizon.

This is particularly true in the field of criminal justice. No American president, no matter how charismatic, no matter how large his or her margin of victory, can alter the direction of the criminal justice system overnight. No idea, no matter how visionary, no matter how intuitively appealing, can automatically overturn decades of accepted thinking and practice across the country.

By its very nature, the criminal justice system in the United States favors incremental, piecemeal, and local reform. If we hope to achieve big goals like reduced crime and incarceration, we must pursue them county by county, agency by agency, block by block.

This collection of essays is a series of extended riffs on this idea. *Reducing Crime, Reducing Incarceration* is an immodest title for a book with a modest agenda: to make the case that small improvements can often add up to big change.

In particular, *Reducing Crime, Reducing Incarceration* takes up a series of questions that have occupied my thinking and my professional career for the past two decades: How do you translate ideas into action at the local level? How do you launch a new criminal justice reform? How do you measure impact? Is it possible to spread new practices to resistant audiences? And what's the point of small-bore experimentation anyway?

Reducing Crime, Reducing Incarceration attempts to answer these questions first through the prism of the Red Hook Community Justice Center, an experimental courthouse in southwest Brooklyn. Viewed critically, the Justice Center is a tiny project, working with a few thousand minor of-

fenders each year in a largely unknown part of New York City. By telling the
Red Hook story in some detail, I hope to show that even relatively small-
scale experiments are enormously difficult to implement. But despite (because of?) this difficulty, small experiments can also reap significant results:
independent evaluators from the National Center for State Courts have
documented that the Justice Center has succeeded in reducing the number
of defendants who receive jail sentences and reducing the number who re-
offend as well. And the neighborhood of Red Hook, once infamous as a site
of drugs and violence, is now a destination for tourists and new businesses.

Next, the book widens its lens to take in the national movement toward
problem-solving justice. Since the launch of the first drug court in Miami,
Florida in the late 1980s, American courts have created thousands of special
initiatives designed to improve the way that judges deal with difficult cases.
The Red Hook Community Justice Center is just one example of a broader
phenomenon that includes mental health courts, domestic violence courts,
veterans courts and numerous variations on these themes. In the second
section of the book, I attempt to define the meaning of problem-solving
justice, to explore how problem-solving courts challenge conventional practice in the courts, and to answer some of the most persistent criticisms these
reforms have engendered.

By and large, the track record of problem-solving courts is solid—there
are numerous studies that document the effectiveness of drug courts in reducing substance abuse, of mental health courts in reducing re-arrests, and
of domestic violence courts in strengthening the supervision of offenders.
This does not mean that all problem-solving courts are successful, however.
Indeed, there are plenty of examples where problem-solving reformers have
struggled to achieve their goals. Part Three of the book looks at this phenomenon and attempts to explore the challenges of effective implementation. One of the implicit messages of this section is that good ideas (and
good intentions) are not enough—real thought must be devoted to how to
adapt to conditions on the ground and how to manage change over the long
haul.

Finally, *Reducing Crime, Reducing Incarceration* turns to the question
of measuring success. The final two chapters attempt to reflect on a generation's worth of criminal justice reform, first in New York City, and then
among problem-solving courts nationally. In essence, these chapters are an
argument that changes in ground-level practice—new training for judges,
shifts in police strategy, investments in evidence-based treatment interventions—can help make a meaningful dent in crime and incarceration rates,
even without wholesale changes to the legal or intellectual frameworks that
underpin the criminal justice system.

In making this case, I am also, by extension, telling the story of the Center for Court Innovation, the public-private partnership where I have worked since the early 1990s. Starting under the leadership of John Feinblatt, the Center for Court Innovation has sought to reform the justice system not through impact litigation or high-profile legislation or political protest, but rather through conceiving and implementing a series of demonstration projects that tweak practice on the ground—and then by disseminating these practices as broadly as possible.

There are frustrations to this approach, to be sure. It is unglamorous. The spread of ideas from successful demonstration projects to the rest of the system is always uneven. And to have any kind of an impact takes years.

But anyone who has visited New York recently can attest that it is a safer place today than it was 20 years ago—a change that has been accomplished without increasing the rate of incarceration. And any close observer of American courts can testify that problem-solving courts are here to stay and have altered not just the way state courts operate but the way they are viewed by the public. The Center for Court Innovation has played a small, supporting role in these changes. *Reducing Crime, Reducing Incarceration* traces the arc of these developments, offering a detailed roadmap for anyone interested in following a similar path.

PART I

COMMUNITY JUSTICE
IN RED HOOK

1 Innovation in Brooklyn: Planning the Red Hook Community Justice Center

How does a new criminal justice program move from concept to implementation? How do you win over skeptical audiences, both within the criminal justice system and out in the community? This essay is the product of a planning diary that I wrote during the early development of the Red Hook Community Justice Center, an experimental courthouse in southwest Brooklyn. It offers a snapshot from the crucial initial stages of planning, including fundraising, program development, and site selection. It was originally written in 1998. I have made some small tweaks to enhance accuracy and reflect recent changes at the Justice Center.

How Did I Get Here?

I remember the first time I ever heard of Red Hook. It was 1991. Against my better judgment, I was dragged by a couple of friends to one of those movie theatres that plays only artsy and independent films. The film showing that day was called "Straight Out of Brooklyn." At the time, I thought it was the most depressing movie I had ever seen. It depicted the struggles of a young man living in public housing in Red Hook and dealing with an extremely dysfunctional family. I don't recall much of the plot, but I do remember that it ended with gunshots and heartache.

So three years later, when I got a call from John Feinblatt, the director of the Center for Court Innovation, asking if I was interested in planning a community court that would attempt to reduce crime in Red Hook, I reacted with no small amount of trepidation. For me, like many New Yorkers, Red Hook conjured up images of a neighborhood under siege, a community that epitomized urban blight and disorder.[1]

---

[1] Here's a typical assessment of the neighborhood: "Fear, drugs and guns have been part of the Red Hook landscape as much as the towering rows of red-brick apartment towers that line the housing project mall." David Gonzalez. "Life in Brooklyn's Forgotten Section; In Red Hook, 3-Year-Olds Hear Gunfire and Duck for Cover," *The New York Times,* December 20, 1992.

While I mulled over John's offer, I went to spend some time in the neighborhood. I expected to see a desolate ghost town, but it didn't take long for me to realize that there was more to Red Hook than its reputation suggested. I visited Red Hook on a beautiful summer day. I walked through Coffey Park, the central neighborhood park, and saw families enjoying the afternoon sun. I toured Red Hook's waterfront, with its spectacular views of the Statue of Liberty and lower Manhattan. I saw visible signs of economic development—a warehouse had been refurbished and an art gallery and small waterfront museum were in the works. Finally, I met a couple of people, most notably Monsignor John Waldron, the parish priest of the local Catholic church, who talked enthusiastically about the neighborhood's rich history and its recent progress in improving the quality of life. By the end of the day, I was sold. I took the job and began what has been one of the most fascinating experiences of my professional life.

Why Red Hook?

In 1992, Patrick Daly, a local school principal, was accidentally murdered in broad daylight when he was mistakenly caught in a shoot-out between rival drug dealers. In the months following his death, then-Brooklyn District Attorney Charles J. Hynes said that he wanted to do more than just prosecute the two shooters; he wanted to make a long-term investment in preventing crime in Red Hook. He told the local media that Red Hook would be an ideal location for a community court that would forge a new response to minor offending, offering community restitution and social services to defendants instead of jail sentences.

Hynes' remarks started the ball rolling, but there were other factors that made Red Hook an attractive site. Most important was the neighborhood's isolation—it is one of the few communities in New York with easily identifiable borders. You know when you're in the neighborhood and you know when you're not. In a well-defined community like Red Hook, it is easier for a demonstration project to have a concentrated impact. It is also simpler for researchers to measure that impact.

By the middle of 1994, the District Attorney's Office and the Center for Court Innovation had agreed that it was worth exploring the feasibility of a community court in Red Hook. The next question was how to proceed. The two offices decided to seek funding to support a feasibility study. The first target was the New York City Housing Authority. This made perfect sense: after all, the majority of Red Hook's residents live in public housing, so the Housing Authority is naturally one of the largest stakeholders in the community. The proposal was successful; it was this grant that enabled the Center for Court Innovation to hire me as the lead planner in the summer of 1994.

Defining the Problem

One of the very first things that happened after I accepted the job was a series of focus groups with Red Hook residents. The Brooklyn District Attorney's Office helped put the groups together, bringing in an outside consultant to facilitate the conversations. We held separate discussions with community leaders, social service providers, young people and single moms. Red Hook is small enough—officially, it has less than 11,000 residents—that we were able to get just about all of the major players in the neighborhood to come, along with many of their constituents. More than 50 people attended the groups, which were held at the Red Hook Public Library. Participants were asked a series of fairly simple questions: What are the major problems in Red Hook? How might a neighborhood court help address them? What should be the court's priorities? The conversations were extremely lively. I remember that once people started talking it was difficult to get them to stop—several of the groups ran well over their allotted times.

I learned a couple of important things from the focus groups. The first was that despite Red Hook's reputation for drugs and serious violence, quality-of-life conditions—graffiti, littering, noise violations, loitering—weighed heavily on the minds of local residents. I remember one participant saying, "Violations do not receive any priority.... We need a [better] quality of life. Even the schools are not safe." Another expressed the feelings of many when he said: "The court system has failed us.... [Offenders] go through revolving doors." [2]

But low-level offending was not the only thing on the minds of the focus group participants. Red Hook residents had problems that took them to Family Court and Civil Court as well as Criminal Court. These included disputes with landlords, small claims cases, and domestic violence issues. Several participants lamented the jurisdictional boundaries of New York's court system. One person said, "You can't divide a person up. You have to have a comprehensive look at the whole person. The community court could do that." Comments like this one confirmed our initial hunch that a community court in a neighborhood like Red Hook should be multi-jurisdictional and that it should attempt to address the full range of legal issues faced by local residents, not just criminal matters.

Finally, participants in the focus groups urged the court to be as aggressive as possible in providing social services. One recommended that the court look at "the total picture—spousal abuse, victim services, teenagers, mentor programs, mock court, parenting skills." From comments like these, we began to fashion a notion that the court should provide services not just

---

[2] All quotations from the focus groups are taken from: Joan E. Jacoby and Edward C. Ratledge. *Community Expectations About the Red Hook Community Court and Justice Center*, Jefferson Institute for Justice Studies, 1994.

to defendants, but to everyone who is touched by crime in Red Hook—defendants, victims and those in the community who are simply concerned about public safety. It was not long after the focus groups that we decided to call the project a "community justice center" instead of a community court. We thought that "community justice center" better signified our intention to build much more than just a courtroom in Red Hook.

Engaging the Community

The focus groups were productive sessions, unearthing a treasure trove of valuable data about community attitudes and expectations. At the same time, they were a useful tool for building neighborhood support, as I discovered in the days that followed. Red Hook is a neighborhood with a deep skepticism about government initiatives, a skepticism that is rooted in a history of government neglect and unwanted intervention. Many Red Hook residents feel that their community is home to a disproportionate number of undesirable government projects. They point to the neighborhood's methadone clinic and waste transfer station as prime examples. They also argue that their neighborhood's character was forever changed for the worse by Robert Moses, the master builder of New York, who essentially cut the neighborhood off from the rest of Brooklyn when he oversaw the construction of the elevated Gowanus Parkway in the 1940s.

Given this history, it is fair to say that many Red Hookers are hesitant about ambitious new government initiatives, no matter how good they sound on paper. In attempting to win community support for the Justice Center, this attitude would prove to be our largest obstacle. We got off to a good start in overcoming it with the focus groups. Almost by accident, we had sent a powerful message to Red Hook residents by convening the focus groups. And that message was: your voice counts. The focus groups were a visible sign that we intended to consult the community at each step of the process. This was not lost on participants.

Over the next several months, I met individually with every stakeholder that I could think of: business owners, clergy, tenant leaders, elected officials, police officers, Housing Authority administrators, local social service providers and others. As an outsider to the community, I took pains to emphasize that I was there to learn from them, that my job was to help translate their concerns and their ideas into concrete programs. In general, people were generous with their time and grateful to be asked about their opinions.

I also went to as many public meetings in Red Hook as possible. At some, I spoke about the Justice Center. At others, I just listened. This sent the message that I wasn't coming to the community as a carpetbagger, that I was interested in more than just selling a bill of goods.

What I learned from all of these encounters was that there is no substitute for face time. In other words, it is impossible to build meaningful relationships without investing significant time and energy. As the months passed, I found my connections with community leaders deepening. I met their children, attended their church services, wrote them letters of recommendation, ate dinner with them, and supported several of their neighborhood charity efforts. These ties would serve the Justice Center well when it was necessary to mobilize neighborhood support for a grant proposal, a newspaper article, or a public meeting.

To my surprise, my outreach efforts revealed very few concerns about the Justice Center. The issues that I did hear were less about the concept than about the process: Who would direct the Justice Center once it opened? What were we doing about jobs for neighborhood residents? Would the Justice Center have a community advisory board?

Given these concerns, we decided to create a formal vehicle for community input. New York City has a network of 59 community boards that are responsible for advising the city's administration about land-use and other neighborhood issues. Several dozen community representatives sit on each board. Early on, Community Board 6 in Brooklyn, which includes Red Hook, agreed to convene a special task force devoted to the Justice Center.

Throughout the planning process, this task force functioned as a de facto advisory board for the project. They convened public meetings about the project every three months or so. These sessions were a valuable opportunity for community residents to stay informed about the Justice Center and for us to keep our fingers on the pulse of the neighborhood.

Building Partnerships

I was not alone in trying to build community support for the Justice Center; from the start, I enjoyed the active partnership of the Brooklyn District Attorney's Office. Charles Hynes' early endorsement lent the project immediate credibility and opened many doors that might otherwise have remained closed. And his decision to dedicate two attorneys—Gene Lopez and Carl Thomas—to the project strengthened the planning team considerably.

I think it is important to note that the partnership with the D.A.'s Office was not a make-believe or paper partnership, but a real-world relationship fraught with real-world tensions and conflicts. Although we shared a common goal—creating a neighborhood justice center—we both had our own organizational agendas and pressures outside of Red Hook. Inter-agency collaboration takes patience, but in my experience it is well worth the effort. The D.A.'s Office helped enrich the planning process, bringing additional resources and a different institutional perspective to the table.

While the relationship with the D.A.'s Office was the most intimate, it was by no means the only partnership that was forged in the early days of the project. Another crucial partner was Safe Horizon, New York's largest victim assistance agency, which runs programs throughout the city's neighborhoods, including Red Hook.

Bringing Safe Horizon into the planning process made perfect sense. After all, a door-to-door survey of neighborhood residents had revealed high levels of fear—nearly seven out of ten respondents said they felt unsafe at their local subway. In this environment, a community justice center would have to be aggressive about providing victims with assistance and giving them a voice in the justice process. Jeanne Mullgrav and Paula Calby at Safe Horizon were instrumental in helping us identify and think through these issues.

Red Hook Public Safety Corps

The most visible sign of our partnership with the D.A.'s Office and Safe Horizon was a joint project launched in the fall of 1995—an AmeriCorps program that put 50 local residents to work on crime prevention and victim assistance projects. In many respects, the AmeriCorps project in Red Hook embodied the values of the Justice Center: it sought to provide an under-served neighborhood with the tools it needs to address disorder and improve public safety.

The AmeriCorps program grew out of a desire to find aggressive and creative ways to solve community problems in Red Hook. The Red Hook Community Justice Center is dedicated to the idea that courts can do more than just respond to crime after it occurs. This means engaging in activities like reaching out to victims, cleaning up local eyesores, and fixing broken windows. But to get this kind of work done requires manpower—manpower that most courts simply do not have.

Luckily, we found a vehicle capable of providing us with the resources we needed. The federal AmeriCorps program provides participants with a small living allowance and an educational award in return for a year's worth of community service work. In 1995, in collaboration with the D.A.'s Office, Safe Horizon, and the National Organization for Victim Assistance, we applied for an AmeriCorps grant, requesting funding to support 50 national service volunteers (and four staff members) in Red Hook.

AmeriCorps turned out to be a perfect fit. The AmeriCorps grant enabled us to establish an ongoing presence in the neighborhood. I was able to use the grant as leverage with the New York City Housing Authority, which donated a ground floor apartment in the Red Hook Houses to serve as our home base. Each day from this headquarters, Corps members spread out across the neighborhood, performing community service at local schools, health clinics, police precincts, and senior centers.

In spirit, the Corps was somewhere between summer camp and boot camp. Our Corps members were bursting with energy and ideas. The challenge was to channel their enthusiasm in productive directions. The easiest way to do this was to give Corps members a role in creating their own service projects. In the process, Corps members pushed the program in some unexpected directions. For example, one member put together a weekend baseball league to keep young people off of the streets. Some observers may fairly question whether running a youth baseball league is an appropriate activity for a court. But this type of engagement with the neighborhood is at the heart of the Red Hook enterprise and is entirely consistent with the Justice Center's commitment to improving the local quality of life.

Our AmeriCorps program was unique in a couple of other respects as well. Unlike many other programs, which parachute volunteers from Ivy League colleges into poor communities, our Corps members were recruited from Red Hook and surrounding neighborhoods. In the program's first year, more than 75 percent of the members were residents of Red Hook's public housing development. In addition, our Corps was inter-generational, with participants ranging in age from 18 to 68. Most AmeriCorps programs are geared toward young people, particularly recent college graduates. Given Red Hook's high rate of unemployment, it came as little surprise that residents of all ages applied to participate in the program.

Over the last couple of years, our AmeriCorps program has undergone several changes in size and scope. But one thing that remains constant is its impact on participants, who are given a chance to broaden their horizons and learn meaningful work skills. Phone surveys with program graduates reveal that many have gone on to full-time employment in the public interest sector, including several who have gone on to work at the Center for Court Innovation.

More importantly, the Corps has made a visible difference in Red Hook, contributing hundreds of thousands of hours of labor to the community. Community leaders in particular have come to see the Corps as a valuable tool, calling on members to help them in implementing projects like community gardens, after-school tutoring, and tenant patrols.

Developing the Site

Beyond its intrinsic value to the community, the Corps served another important purpose: it kept talk of the Justice Center alive when progress was slow. We faced numerous obstacles in developing the Justice Center, but the two most significant were problems with the proposed location and the challenge of raising capital funds. As time went on, these two issues became inextricably connected.

Finding a location for a new project is almost always a tricky business, particularly in a city like New York, where real estate is an extremely precious—and political—commodity. Thankfully, Red Hook offered one major advantage in this regard. Because of the dramatic population and business flight out of the neighborhood over the preceding 25 years, Red Hook had a number of vacant and abandoned properties. After investigating all of the city-owned sites in the neighborhood—and inspecting several privately-held properties as well—eight sites emerged as viable options. Each was close to public transportation and each was large enough to house both a courtroom and social service programs.

In an effort to narrow the list further, we organized a bus tour for local community leaders from the Community Board 6 task force. After looking at all of the possibilities, their clear first choice was Visitation School, a vacant parochial school that had closed its doors in the 1970s.

Visitation struck their fancy for several reasons. First, it was located in between "the front" and "the back." In Red Hook parlance, "the front" signifies the public housing development. "The back" is the area closer to the waterfront, which is composed of single-family row houses that are occupied primarily by Italian and Irish Americans. Visitation, in effect, is situated in neutral territory—it "belongs" to neither the front nor the back. This is an important political consideration in Red Hook.

On an emotional level, many residents were drawn to Visitation because it had once been an important community resource. They looked at the Justice Center as an opportunity to bring back to life a magnificent old building. And magnificent is precisely the word to describe it: built at the turn of the century, Visitation School has the kind of dignified street presence that you might expect from a neighborhood courthouse. And, as it turned out, Catholic Charities, which owned the building, was willing to lease it and play an active role in making the project happen. End of story, right? Wrong.

Visitation was not without its drawbacks. Although the structure itself was in good shape, the interior was a disaster. Asbestos and lead paint were major problems. The roof needed to be replaced. None of the windows were worth saving.

It took several months to investigate the building properly—conducting tests, analyzing results, meeting with engineers and construction managers, preparing preliminary architectural drawings. After all was said and done, we got the bad news: it would cost several million dollars to renovate the building.

Fundraising

Many good ideas founder on the shoals of poor fundraising. No program, no matter how well-intentioned or creative, can survive without adequate resources. I won't lie about this: raising money for the Justice Center was not easy. There were days, even months, when I thought that the project would wither on the vine as we waited for grant proposals to be reviewed.

In addition to the New York City Housing Authority, initial seed money for the Justice Center had been provided by a couple of local foundations—the Shubert Foundation, the Fund for the City of New York, and the Scherman Foundation. While this was enough to keep me employed, it was not nearly enough to support a multi-million dollar renovation project. The question quickly became: where do we find that kind of dough?

The answer came at the end of 1996. After several months of conversations, site visits and proposal writing, we received a grant from the U.S. Department of Justice's Bureau of Justice Assistance to pay for the soft costs associated with renovating the Visitation School—primarily fees for architects, engineers and renovation managers. With this money in hand, we were able to make a much stronger case to the mayor's office in New York. Red Hook all of a sudden had attracted the interest of the federal government, which had shown its commitment to the project by making a multi-year grant. Would the city step up to the plate as well?

This decision was made at the highest possible levels: New York State Chief Judge Judith S. Kaye and New York City Mayor Rudolph Giuliani were personally involved in the conversations. Finally, after more than two years of reaching out to the community, building the concept and developing the site, in December of 1996 the city announced that it would cover the full cost of renovation. The next phase of planning the Justice Center was ready to begin.

Conclusion

A groundbreaking ceremony for the Red Hook Community Justice Center was held in front of Visitation School in the summer of 1998. Several hundred local residents watched as Mayor Rudolph Giuliani, Chief Judge Judith S. Kaye, District Attorney Charles J. Hynes and other dignitaries shoveled the first ceremonial pile of dirt. Before construction could begin, the project had to pass a rigorous community review process that included the local community board, the Brooklyn Borough President and the City Planning Commission. Thanks to the groundwork that had been performed during early planning, the Justice Center passed each stage of review without objection. After two years of construction, the Justice Center officially opened its doors for business in early 2000.

2 Building Legitimacy: Court and Community in Red Hook

This chapter is an effort to tell the story of the operations of the Red Hook Community Justice Center and its relationship with the local community. The goal is to tease out the tension between the two sides of the Justice Center's identity—"community" and "justice"— and to articulate the lessons that the Justice Center's model of neighborhood engagement offers to other neighborhoods and other fields of endeavor such as health care, education, and the environment.

This essay originally appeared in the Justice System Journal (Volume 26, No. 1) in 2005 under the title "Justice in Red Hook" and was co-written by Aubrey Fox, a colleague of mine at the Center for Court Innovation. In revising it for inclusion in this collection, I have removed duplicative material and added new sections to bring it up to date with recent developments in Red Hook.

Introduction

Red Hook is a low-income neighborhood in southwest Brooklyn with a complicated and often unhappy history with local government. In addition to being home to one of New York's oldest and largest public housing projects, Red Hook was cut off from the rest of Brooklyn by the construction of an elevated highway built by Robert Moses in the 1940s over neighborhood protests.

In recent years, Red Hook residents have resisted, through a variety of formal and informal means, neighborhood projects they have not wanted. On thirteen separate occasions, plans to open a waste transfer station in Red Hook have been defeated by organized community opposition.[3] An attempt to create a Business Improvement District never made it past the

---

[3] Anne Raver. "Up from the Ruins, Red Hook Faces a Dump," *The New York Times*, October 1, 1998.

17

local community board.[4] And an artificial turf soccer field donated to Red Hook by the government of Norway was set aflame and destroyed after only ten days of use, according to the *New York Times*.[5]

Like most neighborhoods, Red Hook is not a monolithic, homogenous community. Although the majority of local residents are black and Latino, Red Hook contains several distinct sub-populations and interest groups: public housing tenants, industrial business owners, artists, private homeowners, and real estate developers. Disputes among these groups have often burst into public view, most notably in recent years over waterfront development plans for large box stores (Ikea, Fairway) that have pitted public housing residents interested in job development against single-family homeowners concerned about traffic and congestion. Residents have even fought over what to call the neighborhood, with some trying (unsuccessfully) to change the name to "Liberty Heights" to avoid Red Hook's reputation for drugs, crime and disorder.

There are, however, exceptions to this history of neighborhood fragmentation and resistance to new ideas. The Red Hook Community Justice Center is one example. In the Spring of 2000, the Red Hook Community Justice Center began operations in a refurbished Catholic school just off Red Hook's central park. The Justice Center offers a coordinated approach to criminal, civil and family problems typically addressed in multiple, fragmented courthouses. A single judge hears cases involving quality-of-life crimes, domestic violence and landlord-tenant disputes that would under ordinary circumstances go to three different courts. Offenders and litigants are linked to a wide range of on-site services—drug treatment, job training, GED classes—and mandated to pay back the neighborhood through visible community restitution projects, such as painting over graffiti, cleaning local parks and fixing broken windows. At the same time, the Justice Center is the hub for an array of unconventional programs that engage local residents in community volunteering, youth development, and employment programs.

Before opening its doors, the Justice Center went through an arduous six-year planning process that included formal public review and democratic approval by the local community board, the Brooklyn Borough President and the New York City Planning Commission, as well as extensive consultation with local residents through focus groups, town hall meetings and individual interviews. Thirteen years into operation, the Justice Center enjoys widespread community recognition and support. A 2009 study found that 94 percent of residents had positive feelings towards a community court in

---

[4] Joe Sexton. "Standoff Over Red Hook Renewal: Businesses Fear a Plan to Remake Neighborhood," *The New York Times*, January 5, 1996.

[5] Joe Sexton. "In Red Hook, No Field, No Dreams; A Gift for Children Came From Norway. Vandals Destroyed It," *The New York Times*, September 24, 1994.

their neighborhood.[6] This is in stark contrast to the 10 percent of Red Hook residents who rated the courts positively in a similar survey completed before the Justice Center opened.[7] Approval ratings for criminal justice agencies in general have also increased in Red Hook.

How has the Justice Center managed to achieve these numbers? Why was the Justice Center—a criminal justice project that, among other things, keeps offenders in the neighborhood—approved by the Red Hook community when so many other projects have been rejected? How has the Justice Center navigated the various factions that comprise Red Hook? These are just a few of the questions that the Justice Center raises for those interested in the relationship between government and citizens.

Neighborhood Outreach

The Red Hook Community Justice Center was born out of tragedy. In the early 1990s, Patrick Daly, a school principal, was murdered in a drug-related shoot-out. Soon after, Brooklyn District Attorney Charles Hynes began exploring the idea of launching a new public safety initiative in Red Hook. On the heels of the successful implementation of the Midtown Community Court in 1993, the Center for Court Innovation was asked to investigate the possibility of opening a community court for southwest Brooklyn.

With the backing of Hynes and New York State Chief Judge Judith Kaye, the Center for Court Innovation embarked upon a comprehensive planning process in Red Hook to explore whether a community court might be a feasible solution to some of Red Hook's public safety problems.[8] Our planning team quickly realized that earning the trust and confidence of local residents would be no easy task. At the time the planning process began, Red Hook's population had fallen from over 20,000 people in the 1950s to less than 11,000 according to 1990 census figures.[9] The median household income in Red Hook was $9,500 (far below the city median of $30,000); more than 78 percent of the children in Red Hook lived in households lacking one or both parents; only 6 percent of residents over 25 had college degrees; and over 30 percent of the working-age men in Red Hook were

---

[6] Rachel Swaner. "Community Perceptions of Red Hook, Brooklyn: Views of Quality of Life, Safety, and Services." *Center for Court Innovation* (March 2010), p. 3.

[7] Leslie Paik. "Surveying Communities: A Guide for Community Justice Planners," *U.S. Department of Justice* (May 2003), p. 6.

[8] In addition to myself, the planning team included numerous other people who helped think through the program and the politics of implementation. I will no doubt forget to mention someone, but I would be remiss if I didn't acknowledge the following: John Feinblatt, Adam Mansky, Robert Feldstein, Amanda Burden, Al Siegel, Eric Lee, Michele Sviridoff, David Karnovsky, Tico Taussig, and Leslie Paik.

[9] Community Board 6, "Red Hook: A Plan for Community Regeneration," *City Council Resolution No. 1913.* Calendar No. 40 (August 1996), p. 17.

unemployed.[10] Nearly 8,000 of Red Hook's 11,000 residents, or over 70 percent, lived in public housing.

In Red Hook, the sense of distrust and disconnection from city decision-makers ran deep. Recognizing this, we devised a variety of means to solicit neighborhood input. We organized a series of meetings with residents, including focus groups held at the local library with community leaders, social service providers, young people and single mothers—a wide variety of informants that went beyond the 'usual suspects' of established local leaders. We also conducted dozens of individual interviews, organized bus trips to the Midtown Community Court, attended community meetings, and convened town hall-style meetings that attracted hundreds of participants.

These interactions, both formal and informal, provided plenty of opportunities for back-and-forth. We explained what we hoped a community court could achieve in Red Hook: improving the safety of the neighborhood and enhancing the legitimacy of the justice system in the eyes of local residents. Within these parameters, we expressed a willingness to contemplate different programming ideas suggested by the community. Along with this message of openness, we also communicated certain limits: that the Justice Center would be part of the New York court system and subject to the same rules as other courts. This meant that residents wouldn't choose the judge or play prosecutor or vote on sanctions for offenders. We delivered this news clearly and consistently in an effort to avoid misunderstandings, hurt feelings, and neighborhood backlash.

Over the course of our planning process, we learned that Red Hook residents faced a paradox common to many working-class, urban neighborhoods: fear of crime combined with a deep distrust of the criminal justice system. Participants in initial focus groups indicated their desire to reduce neighborhood crime, telling planners that "Red Hook is lawless" and that the principal problems in Red Hook were "lack of knowledge of the law, lack of respect for the law, lack of respect for neighbors."[11] They reported feeling unsafe in public housing lobbies, elevators and hallways, as well as on local streets. The lack of faith in the criminal justice system was particularly striking. One focus group participant put it this way: "the criminal justice system doesn't work here." This anecdotal impression was confirmed by a door-to-door survey in Red Hook, in which no more than 14 percent of respondents gave "excellent" or "very good" ratings to the police, district attorney or the courts.[12]

---

[10] Community Board 6, "Red Hook: A Plan for Community Regeneration," p. 18.

[11] Joan E. Jacoby and Edward C. Ratledge. *Community Expectations About the Red Hook Community Court and Justice Center*. Jefferson Institute for Justice Studies, 1994.

[12] Paik, "Surveying Communities: A Guide for Community Justice Planners," p. 6.

As important as it was, asking local residents for input only got us so far in terms of winning local support. After all, Red Hook residents had heard their fair share of empty promises and ambitious plans that never came to fruition. To sustain local enthusiasm during the long planning and construction process of the Justice Center, we decided it was important to deliver something tangible to the neighborhood. In 1995, we created an AmeriCorps community service program in Red Hook that put 50 area residents to work on local community service projects—including fixing broken locks in the Red Hook's public housing projects (known as the "Red Hook Houses"), providing security at local schools and escorting senior citizens to public transportation. In exchange, after completing 1700 hours of service, members received a small living stipend and an educational grant. The "Red Hook Public Safety Corps" operated out of a ground floor apartment donated by the New York City Housing Authority. Clad in bright red shirts, the Public Safety Corps became a visible neighborhood presence. Perhaps most importantly, the Public Safety Corps was an early win for the Justice Center, building its credibility with a skeptical neighborhood that had seen other government initiatives come and go.

Operations

The Justice Center officially opened in June 2000. Based on the priorities and programming ideas unearthed during the planning stages, the goal of the Justice Center is to help address neighborhood problems such as chronic low-level offending, drugs, juvenile delinquency, domestic violence and landlord-tenant disputes.

The Justice Center seeks to reduce crime by linking offenders to treatment and other social service interventions, by addressing conditions of disorder through community service, and by improving perceptions of fairness (and thus encouraging voluntary adherence to pro-social norms).

What role does the community play in this agenda? The relationship between the Justice Center and local residents is multi-faceted and mutually beneficial. The Justice Center relies on the community for its raison d'etre, its sense of mission and identity. It depends on community residents to serve as the program's eyes and ears, to nominate problems to be addressed and to help identify solutions. Meanwhile, the community relies on the Justice Center for jobs, services, meeting space and the tools and expertise it brings to the task of solving local problems. But this description just scratches the surface. Residents interact with the Justice Center in a variety of capacities:

As advisers. The Justice Center has a community advisory board, composed of more than three dozen community representatives (e.g. tenant leaders, clergy and civic leaders as well as representatives from local institutions like the schools and the police), that meets regularly to inform Justice Center staff about local conditions and propose new programming ideas. For example, at the advisory board's behest, the Justice Center created a summer internship program for local teens.

As evaluators. In addition, the Justice Center turns to residents for regular, ongoing feedback on court operations. Every other year, the Justice Center sponsors a household survey of local residents. The survey is designed to collect three major types of information: how people perceive the Justice Center, how safe they feel in their neighborhood, and what their public safety priorities are. No other court in the country asks these questions on a regular basis.

As problem solvers. The Justice Center seeks to work with community residents to solve discrete safety problems that typically do not result in court cases. The goal is to create collaborative solutions to local problems. For example, in an effort to address crime and disorder in a local park, the Justice Center helped create "Friends of Coffey Park," a group of over 50 residents and community leaders that organizes clean-up efforts and produces cultural events. When Hurricane Sandy hit New York in 2012, the Justice Center was an active participant in relief and rebuilding efforts, helping to reduce tension throughout the long weeks that Red Hook was without normal electrical service.

As co-producers of justice. The Justice Center runs a youth court in which young people (ages 10–15) who have committed low-level offenses like truancy, fare evasion, and disorderly conduct appear in front of a peer court composed entirely of other teenagers from the neighborhood who have been trained to serve as judge, jury and attorneys. The hearings are entirely staffed and led by teens, who mete out sanctions like community service, letters of apology and anger management to their peers. Compliance stands at 80%, well above comparable Family Court rates. These young people are, in effect, establishing and enforcing standards of behavior for their peers. Another recent experiment in Red Hook pursues a similar goal: in 2012, the Justice Center launched a peacemaking project that adopts Native American dispute resolution techniques to cases referred from the court. Local elders—long-time, respected member of the Red Hook community—work directly with troubled young people to come up with creative responses to conflict and misbehavior.

As service recipients. The on-site social services at the Justice Center (some of which are provided by community-based agencies) are available both to court referrals and to community walk-ins. Each year, thousands are mandated to social services and/or community service. The Justice Center also makes drop-in services available to the community free of charge on a voluntary basis. It houses on-site GED classes, a job developer, counseling, mentoring/internships, mediation, and entitlement assistance. The Justice Center also runs a youth baseball league that each year serves hundreds of participants.

As employees. A number of Red Hook residents work as full-time employees at the Justice Center, supervising community service, working with clients in treatment, and overseeing housing initiatives.

In short, the Justice Center has sought to become a responsible institutional citizen in Red Hook. On a daily basis, it attempts to foster informal interactions between court staff and residents. The building's architecture also seeks to encourage a dynamic exchange with local residents. In contrast to the centralized courthouses in each borough of New York City—imposing structures with elaborate security procedures and labyrinthine floor plans—the Justice Center is a three-story building with a welcoming design, highlighted by abundant light and the use of warmer, informal building materials instead of granite and marble. The building uses architecture to send a message of respect and decency rather than intimidation. One small example is that the height of the judge's bench has been reduced to ensure that when offenders approach the bench, they are eye-to-eye with the judge rather than looking up. While this may be a small detail, it's an important symbol of the Justice Center's desire to open its doors to the community. On any given day, a visitor might find dozens of residents in the building—adult students attending GED class, school children being tutored by court officers, or local organizers using conference rooms for meetings.

This type of collegiality also extends past the courthouse doors. Justice Center staff members regularly attend after-hours community meetings, such as police precinct council meetings and tenant councils; a schedule of events is posted prominently at the Justice Center and staff are assigned to make sure that these events are covered. For staff, community engagement is an explicit part of the job description, and no one is spared this duty, including presiding judge Alex Calabrese, who attends many neighborhood meetings to learn more about the context from which court cases emerge. Regular attendance at community meetings becomes an accountability measure in itself—staff expect to hear from community residents if problems aren't addressed from meeting to meeting.

Finally, on countless occasions, staff interact informally with community members. Judge Calabrese, who is greeted regularly picking up lunch at the local deli or on his way home in the evening, likens Red Hook to a "small town" in terms of the amount of regular contact he has with residents. The Justice Center-sponsored youth baseball league was an idea suggested by a local resident, an AmeriCorps member who felt the neighborhood lacked youth recreational opportunities. Court officers, defense attorneys and local prosecutors coach the teams. These examples represent only a fraction of what goes on in Red Hook.

The goal of the Justice Center's engagement with the Red Hook community is to help close the gap that has emerged between the criminal justice system and the community and to restore the justice system's legitimacy in the eyes of the public it exists to serve. The emerging social science research documents that neighborhoods where residents trust each other and have confidence in local institutions are safer than those without such attributes, even holding factors like race and poverty constant.[13] The Red Hook Community Justice Center is testing the extent to which the criminal justice system can spark these kinds of connections.

Boundaries

The Justice Center was intentionally designed to push the boundaries of government-community collaboration. Indeed, its stated goals of improving neighborhood quality of life and public confidence in the justice system set it apart from the judicial norm. However, it is part of a larger community justice movement in which courts, police, probation, prosecutors and public defense organizations across the country have begun to reach out to community members in new ways.[14]

A wide variety of practice and opinion exists under the community justice umbrella. At one end of the continuum are those who seek to alter the balance of power—and the division of labor—between criminal justice agencies and communities. For example, some argue that citizens—not judges—should have authority to sentence and supervise offenders through initiatives such as reparative justice boards.

At the other end of the spectrum are programs that are engaged in community relations rather than new programming. These projects, which might involve sending criminal justice officials to neighborhood meetings or inviting local clergy to participate in a dialogue, can be important, but they run the risk of invoking community for symbolic rather than substantive purposes. Anthropologist Victoria Malkin notes the possibility that collaboration can be a one-way street, with government agencies enjoying the benefits of community support without addressing the "real" issues that residents are concerned with—turning community engagement into a "performance of accountability for public consumption" with little substantive effect.[15]

---

[13] For example, see Robert J. Sampson and Stephen W. Raudenbush. "Disorder in Urban Neighborhoods—Does It Lead to Crime?" *National Institute of Justice* (February 2001).

[14] Greg Berman and Aubrey Fox. "From the Margins to the Mainstream: Community Justice at the Crossroads," 22 *The Justice System Journal* 2 (2001), p. 1.

[15] Victoria Malkin. "Community Courts and the Process of Accountability: Consensus and

The Red Hook Community Justice Center purposefully falls somewhere in between these two extremes. It has sought to find new ways to bring a court and community together. At the same time, it has been careful to draw some clear distinctions, highlighting where the role of the community ends and the formal justice system begins. How does it strike that balance? It has done so by looking to the community to play a significant role in projects outside of the courtroom while preserving the sanctity of the courtroom process.

Visitors who sit in the courtroom in Red Hook are often surprised to discover that every defendant is represented by counsel and that the Brooklyn D.A.'s office prosecutes every misdemeanor case. In a typical week, the majority of the offenders who plead guilty to low-level crimes like drug possession, shoplifting, and prostitution end up receiving alternative sanctions like community restitution, job training or treatment. But a typical week in Red Hook also finds a handful of cases dismissed by the judge. And a typical week also sees a few cases receiving jail sentences, typically for non-compliance with an alternative sanction. What this suggests is that the Justice Center's community orientation has not affected the court's ability to weigh the merits of each case—or the ability of advocates to do their jobs. On the contrary, a problem-solving court like the one in Red Hook gives judges and attorneys the information and sentencing options they need to provide more individualized justice to defendants.

Perhaps the most important thing the Justice Center has done is to make the community the basis for measuring success. The Justice Center works to obtain information about Red Hook's quality of life through crime statistics, door-to-door surveys, intermittent focus groups, and day-to-day interactions with court users. By changing the measure of success—by articulating a clear sense of mission for the court—the Justice Center has profoundly altered the approach of everyone in the building.

Lessons

In Red Hook, an enhanced focus on community participation has not only restored a measure of public trust and confidence in government but has also improved court effectiveness. Put another way, community engagement at the Justice Center isn't just a "feel-good" initiative—it allows the Justice Center to accomplish some important goals that it couldn't otherwise. These include:

Better Decisions. Judge Calabrese and other decision makers make better decisions and get better results when they understand local conditions. For example, unlike many housing court judges who have never seen

---

a public housing project, Judge Calabrese has personally visited public housing units to inspect repairs. The first time Calabrese went on an inspection, the local public housing superintendent told him, "I've been doing this for over 20 years, and I've never seen a judge come to the houses. You must be from the new court." Now the public housing authority is quick to make repairs—in large part because they want to avoid another visit from the judge. Another example of how the judge makes better decisions is seen in trespass cases, which are extremely difficult to adjudicate in a place like Red Hook which has dozens of public housing buildings. Distinguishing legitimate visits to friends and family from illegal attempts to buy drugs is almost impossible. However, Judge Calabrese's knowledge of local conditions—for example, that the building known as the "pharmacy" is a notorious drug den while the one across the street isn't—allows him to make more nuanced decisions about these cases.

Solving Problems. The Justice Center's community ties allow it to solve problems that would otherwise go unaddressed. A few years ago, the Justice Center sought to address a group of abandoned cars that had been illegally dumped in a nearby alley, breeding garbage, rats and other problems. Residents who complained about the problem through the usual channels quickly discovered that no one would take responsibility—not police, not the sanitation department, not the landlords who collectively own the property. Frustrated, several residents brought the problem up to staff at the Justice Center. After a series of brainstorming sessions facilitated by the Justice Center, residents and government officials implemented several solutions. The neighbors pooled together their money to have the cars towed by a private contractor. Further, the neighbors agreed to erect a gate to the alley in an effort to prevent further incidents. And the police promised to monitor the situation closely—and to respond immediately if and when a new car was abandoned in the alley. This is the kind of problem that would never come to an ordinary courthouse; after all, no arrest had been made and no lawsuit had been filed.

Changing Sentencing Practice. The involvement of community residents has pushed the Justice Center to change sentencing practices. The views of Red Hook residents mirror national surveys: while citizens don't want crime to go unpunished, they do (strongly) support alternatives to incarceration that attempt to keep people from returning to court again and again. Through the aggressive use of community restitution and social service mandates, the Justice Center has significantly reduced the number of defendants receiving jail sentences. According to preliminary results from an independent evaluation by the National Center for State Courts, 78 percent of defendants receive alternative sanctions compared to 22 percent in a comparison group that went through Brooklyn's regular criminal court.

And Red Hook reduced the number of defendants receiving jail sentences by 35 percent.[16]

Reducing Re-offending. Most important, recidivism has gone down in Red Hook. The research team documented that juveniles at the Justice Center were 20 percent less likely to re-offend and adults 10 percent less likely than a comparison group whose cases were handled at the regular criminal court in Brooklyn. This finding is particularly noteworthy because the Justice Center tends to work with offenders over only a short period—the typical misdemeanant is sentenced to only a few days of community service rather than months of intensive inpatient drug treatment. The researchers hypothesize that the Justice Center's emphasis on procedural justice helped to change behavior—defendants thought they were treated fairly and respectfully, and thus were more likely to comply with court orders and obey the law.

Improving Accountability. Compliance rates with alternative sanctions at the Red Hook Community Justice Center consistently average 75 percent—a 50 percent improvement on the national standard.[17] Unlike the conventional practice in state criminal courts, Red Hook's presiding judge, Alex Calabrese, actively monitors defendants post-sentence, often requiring them to appear regularly before the bench to report on their progress in treatment or their compliance with other court mandates. Prosecutors, defense attorneys and court staff assigned to the Justice Center work collaboratively with the judge to craft individualized service and treatment plans for each defendant. The idea is that judicial monitoring increases the chances that a defendant will successfully complete their treatment and other sentence mandates and reduces the likelihood of re-arrest.

Access to Services. The Justice Center has shown that it is possible to use a courthouse as a hub for social services. Not only has the Justice Center succeeded in bringing new services like job training, GED classes and drug treatment into an under-resourced neighborhood, it has also demonstrated that it is possible to overcome the stigma of the criminal justice system: each year, hundreds of Red Hook residents seek services voluntarily at the Justice Center.

Reducing Fear. By improving the visibility of justice, the Red Hook Community Justice Center has helped reduce levels of fear in the neighborhood. For example, surveys reveal that since the Justice Center opened, the percentage of Red Hook residents who say they are afraid to go to the parks

---

[16] David Rottman et al. "A Comprehensive Evaluation of the Red Hook Community Justice Center," *National Center for State Courts.* (Publication forthcoming).

[17] "Red Hook Justice." PBS Independent Lens. http://www.pbs.org/independentlens/red-hookjustice/redhook.html

or subway at night has dropped 42 percent.[18]

Legitimacy. Finally, the Justice Center seeks to build institutional legitimacy through its community ties. The crisis of faith in democratic institutions is something to take seriously—it is a real problem when courts are viewed as remote, aloof or racist. For example, surveys of public attitudes towards the courts show that African-Americans are more likely than members of other groups to report that courts are unfair and treat court users with insufficient respect.[19] Without community buy-in, courts can't organize juries, get witnesses to testify or ensure that court orders will be followed. One tangible sign that the Justice Center has had a positive effect on public confidence comes from the 94 percent approval rating it received from local residents in the 2009 neighborhood survey. And support for the Justice Center may have also spilled over into support for other criminal justice institutions—according to door-to-door surveys, approval ratings of police, prosecutors, and judges have increased three-fold since the Justice Center opened. The Justice Center also seems to have improved defendant perceptions of procedural fairness.[20]

Conclusion

In sum, the Justice Center has proven that "community" and "justice" are not in fact oppositional forces. They're not always in perfect harmony, but the truth is that there is significant overlap between the interests of local residents and justice agencies. No resident wants to live in fear, their community overrun by drug dealers. And no criminal justice official wants local residents to view them with suspicion. In truth, everyone has a stake in making the criminal justice system more responsive to neighborhood concerns.

The Justice Center has attempted to mine these areas of goal congruence between government and community, in the process raising some fundamental questions: Does this amount to a new model of democratic governance, or is it simply an example of good government within the existing framework? How important is Red Hook's small scale to the experiment? Is it possible to replicate the Red Hook model in other places, and in other areas of government endeavor?

Red Hook provides an interesting test case for a consideration of how collaboration can produce tangible benefits for both government and community. Red Hook is much changed from 2000 when the Justice Center

---

[18] "Red Hook Community Justice Center: Documented Results." *Center for Court Innovation.* http://www.courtinnovation.org/sites/default/files/RH_Fact_sheet.pdf

[19] David Rottman et al. "Perceptions of the Courts in Your Community: The Influence of Experience, Race and Ethnicity, Executive Summary," *National Center for State Courts* (2003).

[20] Somjen M. Frazer. "Defendant Perceptions of Fairness at the Red Hook Community Justice Center." *U.S. Bureau of Justice Assistance* (September 2006), p. 14.

opened. Crime is down, as are levels of fear. Businesses have moved in. While the Justice Center can't take all the credit for Red Hook's rebirth, it is a significant part of the story. And at the end of the day, given the community's troubled history with government, this is no small accomplishment.

3 Community Court: Common Principles

While the Red Hook Community Justice Center is a particularly ambitious experiment in community justice, it is not the only one of its kind. Indeed, it was preceded by the Midtown Community Court and followed by several dozen projects that have sought to achieve similar goals in disparate locations. This chapter seeks to articulate a set of common principles for community courts. It is based largely on the Center for Court Innovation's work in New York, although it attempts to incorporate other examples as well. I first attempted this exercise back in 1997 in concert with John Feinblatt. I then went back and tried again in 2010. This essay represents my third and hopefully final attempt. In setting out a set of basic principles, my goal was to aid those reformers interested in wholesale replication of community court model and to also encourage the spread of these ideas to mainstream criminal courts.

Introduction

Instead of focusing exclusively on reacting after the fact to individual crimes and offenders, many criminal justice agencies have begun to think more broadly about how to improve public safety and the quality of life in crime-plagued neighborhoods. This process began in the field of policing. Starting a little more than a generation ago, several overlapping reform movements emerged, including broken windows policing, community policing, and problem-oriented policing. In general, advocates of these ideas argued that police officers could address neighborhood crime and disorder more effectively if they established closer relationships with community residents, took low-level crime more seriously, and thought more deeply about how to identify and solve crime patterns as opposed to simply responding to a call for service after a crime had been committed.

From this starting point, these ideas began to spread to other branches of the criminal justice system, including courts. For example, community courts like the Red Hook Community Justice Center seek to improve the judicial response to low-level crime and bolster public trust in justice. In general, community justice programs focus the justice system on two goals: prevention and problem solving. At the end of the day, community justice is about engaging stakeholders like residents, merchants, churches, and schools in seeking to prevent crime before it occurs. And it's about testing new, aggressive, and strategic approaches to public safety when crime happens, particularly low-level offending.

Midtown Community Court

The community court story begins on the streets of midtown Manhattan in the early 1990s. Launched in 1993, the Midtown Community Court represented a dramatic departure from the way that lower courts traditionally have operated in New York City. In the 1960s, New York closed down a network of neighborhood magistrate courts that were responsible for arraigning defendants and disposing of low-level criminal cases. Under the new system, intake and arraignment duties were shifted to centralized courthouses serving each of the city's five boroughs. The change was intended to increase efficiency and deter corruption. These improvements came at a cost however: as courts were removed from the communities they were intended to serve, many New Yorkers lost a visible connection to the justice system.

In the years following the abandonment of the magistrate courts, caseloads increased exponentially, in response to rising crime and an increased focus by law enforcement agencies on quality-of-life offenses such as shoplifting, prostitution, vandalism, and minor drug possession. Judges and attorneys felt enormous pressure to adjudicate cases as quickly as possible. The majority of misdemeanor cases were disposed of during their first appearance in court with only the most cursory legal review—a far cry from a meaningful "day in court."

If the process was far from ideal, so too were the outcomes. All too often, defendants who admitted their guilt to low-level offenses were sentenced to either a few days in jail or to nothing at all—essentially a conditional discharge with no conditions. Neither of these dispositions did much to advance the traditional goals of sentencing: rehabilitation, incapacitation, individual deterrence, or general deterrence. And neither did much to impress local residents and assure community members that their concerns were taken seriously.

No neighborhood was hit harder by quality-of-life crime in the 1970s and 1980s than Times Square. It is sometimes difficult to remember now—

through the prism of two decades of historic crime reductions—but not too long ago, New York City was viewed by many as ungovernable, and Times Square was known for having more low-level crime than any other place in the country.[21] Several Broadway theaters sat empty—no ticket buyers, no shows. Civic leaders such as Gerald Schoenfeld, the head of the Shubert Organization, which owns many Broadway theaters, argued at the time that tourists were being scared away by the neighborhood's reputation for disorder and crime.[22]

Recognizing these problems, a small group of criminal justice planners—led by John Feinblatt and including Michele Sviridoff, Robert Keating, Amanda Burden, Herb Sturz, John Williams, and others—began to advance a novel idea: that a neighborhood-based court, located in Midtown Manhattan and devoted exclusively to handling minor offenses, could do a better job of demonstrating to the local community that the justice system is responsive to local concerns. The planning team spent more than two years on research, program development, and fundraising. In 1993, they revealed the results of their labors.

Located on a busy side street not far from Times Square, the Midtown Community Court occupies a 100-year-old building that was formerly a magistrate courthouse. The planning team put great effort into the physical design of the courthouse, making it complement and reflect the programmatic vision of the experiment. For example, the holding area for defendants featured clean, well-lit areas secured with specially treated glass panels—a marked contrast to the squalid holding pens with iron bars in many urban courthouses. A full floor of office space was devoted to an onsite clinic staffed by social workers and community service supervisors responsible for working directly with defendants. And the building was wired for an innovative computer system that allowed the judge, attorneys, and social service providers to keep in touch with each other and access information about defendants at the click of a mouse.

The location, architecture, and technology were all designed to help the Midtown Community Court address the problem of low-level street crime on the West Side of Manhattan. Misdemeanor defendants at the Midtown Community Court were sentenced to pay back the community they had harmed through visible work projects in the neighborhood—caring for street trees, getting rid of graffiti, and cleaning local parks. At the same time, the court sought to use its legal leverage to link defendants with social services—drug treatment, job training, and counseling—to help address the problems that often fueled criminal behavior. By combining punishment

---

[21] Milton Bracker. "Life on W. 42nd St.: A Study in Decay," *New York Times*, March 14, 1960.

[22] Louis Calta. "Broadway Crime Topic Of Debate: Drama Desk Hears Critics and Supporters of Area," *New York Times*, June 13, 1972, p. 51.

and help, the court sought to stem the chronic offending that was demoralizing local residents, businesses, and tourists.

Evidence suggests that the Midtown Community Court has largely succeeded in its mission. Today, Times Square is a symbol of New York's rebirth—a vibrant crossroads and a prime destination for tourists. Independent evaluators from the National Center for State Courts studied the Midtown Community Court for three years, ultimately producing a book on the experiment called *Dispensing Justice Locally: The Implementation and Effects of the Midtown Community Court*.[23] Among other things, the researchers documented that the project helped to reduce local crime by as much as 56 percent in the case of prostitution. The study also found that the Midtown Community Court improved compliance with court orders— the community service compliance rate was 50 percent higher than other comparable courts. Each year, defendants sentenced by the court performed hundreds of thousands of dollars' worth of community service in the neighborhood. Perhaps as a result, there was a surge of local support for the idea of community justice—two out of three local residents reported that they would be willing to pay additional taxes to support a community court.[24]

In a 2009 *City Journal* essay entitled "How New York Became Safe: The Full Story," one of the original authors of the broken windows theory, George Kelling, addressed the crucial role that the Midtown Community Court played in transforming Times Square: "Sporadic police programs weren't enough. Only when a wide range of agencies and institutions began to work on restoring public order did real progress begin.... The judiciary branch got involved with the 1993 opening of the Midtown Community Court, which swiftly handles those who commit minor offenses."[25] In 2003, looking back at the history of Times Square, New York City Mayor Michael Bloomberg said, "Times Square was [once] seen as the quality-of-life crime capital of the City. Today, it is the heart of New York with thriving commerce, clean streets and packed theaters. The Midtown Community Court brought justice to a problem area and the results couldn't be clearer."[26]

It didn't take long for the results of the Midtown Community Court to attract the attention of policymakers in Washington, D.C. In 1996, the U.S.

---

[23] Richard Curtis et al. *Dispensing Justice Locally: The Impact, Costs and Benefits of The Midtown Community Court*. Harwood Academic Publishers, 2000.

[24] Richard Curtis et al. "Dispensing Justice Locally: The Impact, Costs and Benefits of the Midtown Community Court," *National Criminal Justice Reference Service* (September 2002), pp. 7-13.

[25] George L. Kelling. "How New York Became Safe: The Full Story," *City Journal*, July 17, 2009.

[26] Office of the Mayor. "Mayor Michael R. Bloomberg And New York Chief Judge Judith S. Kaye Celebrate The 10th Anniversary Of The Midtown Community Court," *Press Release* 360-03 (December 15, 2003).

Department of Justice devoted a policy brief to the project, *In New York City, a "Community Court" and a New Legal Culture.*[27] This was soon followed by a visit to Midtown from U.S. Attorney General Janet Reno.

Federal interest advanced the cause in two important ways. First, a grant from the Bureau of Justice Assistance provided the Center for Court Innovation with the resources to disseminate the community court model nationally; these resources were used to create a website, how-to manuals, conferences, and training sessions. Equally important, another federal grant helped to jump-start planning for a second community court in New York, located in Red Hook, Brooklyn.

Red Hook Community Justice Center

Located in a refurbished parochial school, the Red Hook Community Justice Center shares the same basic DNA as the Midtown Community Court; each is a neighborhood-based court that seeks to improve the local quality of life and reengineer the relationship between the justice system and local residents. Within this broad framework, however, there are significant differences, many of which result from differences between the two neighborhoods.

Unlike Midtown Manhattan, which is a central hub of business and tourism, Red Hook, Brooklyn, is an isolated community dominated by one of New York's largest and oldest public housing developments. In Midtown, the population is exceedingly transient; each day, hundreds of thousands of people come into the community from other places across the region and around the world. By contrast, Red Hook is rarely visited by outsiders and most of the crimes committed in the neighborhood feature residents as both victims and perpetrators.

While Times Square is known as the crossroads of the world, Red Hook rarely intrudes on the public consciousness—except when things go terribly wrong. One such moment occurred in 1992, when Patrick Daly, the principal of a local elementary school, was shot to death in a gunfight between two rival drug dealers. In the aftermath of his murder, Brooklyn District Attorney Charles J. Hynes successfully prosecuted both dealers even though forensics could not determine whose bullet ultimately killed Daly.[28]

But Hynes also recognized that traditional law enforcement alone could not solve Red Hook's problems. Just a few years earlier, *Life Magazine* had labeled Red Hook one of the most crack-infested neighborhoods in the country. Hynes argued that addressing Red Hook's problems would

---

[27] David C. Anderson. "In New York City, a 'Community Court' and a New Legal Culture," *U.S. Department of Justice* (February 1996).

[28] Joseph P. Fried. "Youths Guilty In the Slaying of a Principal," *The New York Times*, June 16, 1993.

take more than arrests, prosecutions, and prison sentences. Looking for potential answers, he turned to the idea of a community court.

The community court model that emerged in Red Hook—with the crucial backing and leadership of New York State Chief Judge Judith S. Kaye, Chief Administrative Judge Jonathan Lippman, and the City of New York under Mayor Rudy Giuliani—is a multifaceted one. In addition to hearing low-level criminal cases, the Red Hook judge handles selected juvenile delinquency cases from Family Court and landlord-tenant disputes from Civil Court.

The Justice Center's multi-jurisdictional courtroom acknowledges that the problems faced by citizens often do not conform to the narrow jurisdictional boundaries imposed by modern court systems. Criminal defendants may also be involved in a landlord-tenant dispute or a family court case. Handling all of these cases in the same place enhances the court's ability to get to the root of the problem. As with the Midtown Community Court, the Red Hook courtroom emphasizes finding nontraditional answers to the problems that bring people to court. Functionally, this has meant moving away from incarceration as a default sentence, and moving toward the use of social services—drug treatment, counseling, and job training—and community restitution as a response to criminal behavior.

Under the terms of New York City's stringent land-use process, designed to prevent poor neighborhoods from being burdened with unwanted government programs, the Red Hook Community Justice Center had to be approved by the local community board, the borough president, and the city planning commission before it could open its doors. The Justice Center passed each of these hurdles without a single objection from either a community leader or a local elected official. Given the general unpopularity of criminal justice programs, particularly those that promise to keep defendants in the community, this was a significant accomplishment.

What drove this success? There are many answers. By design, and by circumstance, the planning team for the Justice Center—which I had the pleasure of joining in 1994—spent several years on a thorough community needs assessment process in Red Hook, getting to know the neighborhood and all of the key players. This certainly helped facilitate the approval process.

But the real key was the decision to respond to community input about the program. One of the recurring themes during the needs assessment process was the desire expressed by local residents for the Justice Center to be more than just a courtroom. As a result, we developed a plan for the Justice Center to be the hub for a broad range of unconventional programs targeted at preventing crime, not just responding after it occurs. This vision ultimately came to include an AmeriCorps community service program, a teen-led youth court, a mentoring initiative, health care screening, GED classes, and a teen photography program. Crucially, these programs were available to anyone in the neighborhood who was interested in them, not just those with court cases.

In no small part because the Justice Center incorporated feedback from local residents into its design, the project has had a steady diet of accomplishments since its opening in 2000. It has won numerous awards, including national prizes for innovation from the American Bar Association and the National Criminal Justice Association, and favorable coverage by the mainstream media, including a PBS documentary.[29]

More importantly, the Justice Center has made a difference on the streets of Brooklyn. Like the Midtown Community Court before it, the Red Hook Community Justice Center has succeeded in changing sentencing practices by reducing the use of incarceration. It has also improved compliance with community service mandates, which translates into hundreds of thousands of dollars worth of labor to the neighborhood each year. Surveys reveal that local residents' opinions of the courts and defendants' perceptions of fairness have improved considerably. Independent evaluators from the National Center for State Courts have confirmed that arrests went down (and stayed down) in Red Hook's local precinct after the Justice Center opened—something that was not true in neighboring precincts. They also were able to document reduced re-offending among participants at the Justice Center when compared to other, similarly-placed Brooklyn offenders whose cases were handled in the conventional criminal court in downtown Brooklyn. Red Hook, once notorious for drugs, crime, and disorder, is now home to one of the safest police precincts in Brooklyn, as measured by the number of felony arrests.

Principles

The Midtown and Red Hook community courts have helped to pave the way for dozens of community courts around the world, including those close to home (Harlem, the Bronx, Newark) and those in far-off locations (England, Canada, South Africa, Australia).

Each community court has contributed its own special element to the movement. For example, at the North Liverpool Community Justice Centre, the judge was selected in a formal process overseen by a panel that included local residents—a first for England. The Hartford Community Court in Connecticut was the first to attempt to work citywide rather than in a single neighborhood. In Dallas, Texas, two community courts saved money and

---

[29] "Red Hook Justice." *PBS Independent Lens.* http://www.pbs.org/independentlens/red-hookjustice/redhook.html

strengthened community ties by operating out of preexisting community centers rather than a standalone courthouse.

While each community court is unique, it is possible to identify six common underlying principles that differentiate the kind of problem-solving justice practiced in community courts from standard operating procedure in the justice system: enhanced information, community engagement, collaboration, individualized justice, accountability, and outcomes.

Enhanced Information

Community courts are committed to the idea that better staff training combined with better information—not just about individual defendants, but about the community context of crime—can improve the decision making of judges, attorneys, and other justice officials. For example, the Harlem Community Justice Center uses a validated, evidence-based screening tool to assess criminogenic risks and related needs. High-quality information—gathered with the assistance of technology and shared in accordance with confidentiality laws—can help practitioners make more nuanced decisions about both the treatment needs of individual defendants and the risks they pose to public safety. The goal is to ensure that defendants receive an appropriate level of supervision and services.

Community courts make available as much information as possible to the judge at the defendant's first appearance. This allows the judge to act as a practical problem-solver as well as an imposer of sanctions, matching each defendant with treatment and community service programs. By entering data into a central database simultaneously accessible by the judge, prosecutors, defense attorneys, and social service staff, a community court allows all parties to share information as soon as it is available. Simultaneous access helps disparate agencies work together and limits "gaming" of the system by litigants or their attorneys, who might seek to take advantage of information delays.

Community Engagement

Community courts recognize that neighborhoods can be victims too. As the broken windows theory posits, if left unaddressed, low-level offenses erode communal order, leading to disinvestment and neighborhood decay and creating an environment where more serious crime can flourish.

Community courts seek to offer citizens and neighborhood groups an active voice in doing justice. Local residents have an important role to play in helping the justice system identify, prioritize, and solve local problems.

The operating theory behind community courts is that actively engaging citizens helps improve public trust in the justice system. And, as Professor Tom Tyler has documented in his seminal book *Why People Obey the Law*, people are more likely to obey the law if they believe it is legitimate.[30] In an effort to help people feel safer, foster law-abiding behavior, and make members of the public more willing to cooperate as witnesses and jury members, community courts have sought to make justice visible, putting offenders to work in places where neighbors can see what they are doing and outfitting them in ways that identify them as offenders performing community service.

In addition, community courts welcome observers and visitors. Calendars and other information about courtroom activities are easily accessible to the public. The courthouse staff are prepared to answer questions and give tours. And they are prepared to use data: the best court administrators monitor crime conditions in the community and look for opportunities to involve the community in addressing crime-related problems as they develop.

At San Diego's Beach Area Community Court, for example, volunteers participate in community impact panels in which citizens discuss with low-level offenders the impact of their offenses on neighborhood quality of life.[31] From hosting community events to conducting door-to-door surveys to convening a neighborhood advisory board, community courts can offer local residents a variety of mechanisms for interacting with the judge and court administrators.

Collaboration

Community courts are uniquely positioned to engage a diverse range of people, government agencies, and community organizations in collaborative efforts to improve public safety. By bringing together justice partners (e.g., judges, attorneys, probation officers) and reaching out to potential stakeholders beyond the courthouse (e.g., social service providers, victims groups, schools), community courts seek to improve interagency communication, encourage greater trust between citizens and government, and foster new responses to public safety problems. For example, the Seattle Community Court has an advisory board that brings government and nonprofit partners together to offer feedback and share ideas.[32] Community court staff also regularly attend community meetings and keep partners updated through newsletters.

Too often, criminal justice agencies work in isolation, moving cases from street to court to cell and back again without communicating with one

---

[30] Tom R. Tyler. *Why People Obey the Law*. Princeton University Press, 2006, p. 62.

[31] Sebastian Ruiz. "Community Court Provides Options for Beach Rule-breakers," *San Diego News*, September 27, 2007.

[32] Seattle Community Court, "Community Engagement." http://www.seattle.gov/communitycourt/about/community_engagement.htm

another or taking the time to problem-solve. Because of its role as a central hub in the justice process, a community court can play an important communication and coordination function, helping to reduce this phenomenon.

Even if the justice system works harmoniously, it cannot be expected to solve difficult neighborhood problems by itself. As criminal justice agencies look to play a more aggressive role in addressing complicated issues such as quality-of-life crime, they must also seek out new partners. Social service providers—both community-based organizations and government agencies—can provide valuable expertise, including counseling, job training, drug treatment, and mediation skills.

By locating representatives of multiple agencies under a single roof, community courts encourage social service providers and criminal justice professionals to work together. Judges in a community courthouse can consult with treatment professionals on individual cases. Police can alert counselors to defendants who may be open to receiving help. Clerks can help link individual victims to assistance. Physical proximity makes possible closer and more coordinated working relationships.

Individualized Justice

Standard sentencing in low-level cases—short-term jail, fines, conditional discharges without any meaningful conditions—does little to restore the damage caused by crime. Nor does it do much to prevent an individual from returning to court as a chronic offender.

Instead of simply reproducing business as usual, community courts seek to combine punishment and help. The focus of community courts is on linking defendants to individually tailored, community-based sanctions such as community restitution, job training, and drug treatment. Encouraging individual defendants to deal with their underlying problems (addiction, mental illness, joblessness) has a practical crime-control value: positive changes in offender behavior are directly linked to reducing crime.[33]

Community courts look for ways that sentences can help defendants change their lives. Drug treatment, medical services, educational programs, and counseling can all be incorporated into court orders. In many respects, community courts seek to use a court appearance as a gateway to treatment. The crisis of arrest may prompt a defendant to seek help. A court can use its coercive power and knowledge of available resources to reinforce that impulse.

---

[33] For example, research on drug courts shows that reduced substance abuse leads to reduced recidivism. Mary Murrin and Roger H. Peters. "Effectiveness of Treatment-Based Drug Courts in Reducing Criminal Recidivism," 27 *Criminal Justice & Behavior* 1 (February 2000), pp. 72-96.

In attempting to tailor sentences to each defendant and in emphasizing alternatives to incarceration, community courts seek to help reduce recidivism, improve community safety, and enhance confidence in justice.

Accountability

Community courts seek to send the message that all criminal behavior, even quality-of-life crime, has an impact on community safety—and that there are consequences for breaking the law. For example, the Atlanta Community Court holds low-level quality-of-life offenders accountable by requiring them to perform community service—such as neighborhood cleanups, graffiti removal, and office tasks—in the neighborhood where the offense occurred.[34]

By insisting on regular and rigorous compliance monitoring and clear consequences for noncompliance, community courts work to improve the accountability of low-level offenders. One of the most basic tools in a community court judge's arsenal is requiring defendants to come back to court to provide updates on their progress in alternative sanctions. Regular reports can also improve the accountability of service providers, who know that their work will be under public scrutiny. Compliance appearances allow the judge to recognize problems as they develop—and to move aggressively to address them. They also send a message—both to other defendants and the members of the general public who attend court—that community court sanctions are meaningful.

As in drug courts, judges in community court use both positive reinforcement and threat of punishment to motivate defendant compliance. Positively acknowledging compliance is as important as punishing failure. Graduation ceremonies in the courtroom or even a simple handshake from the judge can be a powerful motivator to defendants as they attempt to get their lives on track.

Outcomes

At a community court, the active collection and analysis of data—measuring outcomes and process, costs and benefits—are crucial tools for evaluating the effectiveness of operations and encouraging continuous improvement. For example, Bronx Community Solutions has a researcher who measures compliance rates and other variables, providing regular feedback to staff. In one instance, the researcher found that approximately 15 percent of individuals sentenced to perform alternative sanctions never made it from the courtroom to the intake office. Based on this information, program admin-

---

[34] "Interview: Phillip McDonald, Court Administrator, Atlanta Community Court," *Center for Court Innovation.* http://www.courtinnovation.org/research/phillip-mcdonald-court-programs-administrator-atlanta-community-court?url=research%2F4%2Finterview&mode=4&type=interview&page=1

istrators instituted an escort system that relies on AmeriCorps members to walk participants from the courtroom to the intake office.

A community court seeks to move beyond the standard units of measurement used to assess court performance. In all too many places, courts are asked only to report on volume and speed: how many cases were processed and how quickly? While these results are important and should be tracked, community courts seek to add additional questions to the list, including: What impact did the court have on local quality of life? Do defendants think that their cases were handled fairly? How do local residents perceive the court?

Community courts' use of research is based on a simple premise: by changing the questions asked of the justice system, it is often possible to change the behavior of those who work within the system.

Public dissemination of community court research can be a valuable symbol of public accountability, offering tangible evidence to local residents that the justice system is attempting to address their concerns and solve public safety problems.

Obstacles

Developing a community court is a complex undertaking. While it is almost impossible to predict all of the challenges community court planners will confront, there are several potential obstacles that stand out.

By definition, community courts embrace a variety of stakeholders. These include not only judges, police officials, defense attorneys and prosecutors, but also tenant groups, victims' organizations, businesses, schools, and block associations. Reaching outside the walls of the justice system to involve new players and create new partnerships can complicate both planning and implementation. Many criminal justice officials are not trained for this specific type of work. Moreover, there is the problem of defining roles, responsibilities, and boundaries. Community leaders will understandably expect to have substantive involvement in a community court, but there are always going to be decisions that must be made by professionals alone. Figuring out where to draw this line—and then communicating it in a way that everyone involved understands—is crucial to the ultimate success of a community court.

While the need to bridge the gap between communities and courts may seem self-evident, there are legitimate reasons why many judges, attorneys, and police officers don't reach out to the community in a systematic way. Many criminal justice players believe that greater involvement with the community will compromise their objectivity. In an effort to maintain impartiality, judges have traditionally insulated themselves from the communities and victims affected by the issues they adjudicate, while district attorneys and police departments have restricted the discretion of frontline attorneys and officers on the beat. In addition, many criminal justice professionals feel too overwhelmed by the daily pressures of their jobs to reach out to the community. They are reluctant to take on new responsibilities when they are unsure they will receive the tools they need to get the job done. Community court planners can go at least part of the way to overcoming these objections by linking reluctant judges and attorneys to their peers in other jurisdictions that have managed to navigate these same issues.

In addition to concerns about independence and workload, some criminal justice agencies may be uncomfortable working with social service providers. After all, the underlying assumptions and guiding philosophies of law enforcement and social work differ in fundamental ways. Criminal justice professionals are accustomed to a system of escalating sanctions in which defendants are punished more severely each time they fail; criminal courts are not usually in the business of giving offenders a second chance. Treatment professionals, on the other hand, expect relapses and consider it critical that clients remain in treatment regardless. Addicts may have to hear the same message several times before it finally sinks in. A community court's approach can work only if criminal justice and social service professionals are willing to adjust their outlooks and work in a coordinated way.

Providing timely and accurate information to courtroom decision makers is another key challenge. Although many criminal justice agencies are automated, their computers are rarely designed for courtroom use. Information managers typically organize and track transactions after they occur, rather than using information to improve the quality of decision-making as it takes place. In addition, courtroom decisions often hinge on information maintained by different agencies—police, probation, social services, the court—whose computer hardware and software may not be compatible. Only through vigorous collaborative planning can these kinds of concerns be overcome.

Finally, there is the problem of money. It is difficult to open a community court without some new resources. Even if a jurisdiction decides to forego the costs associated with a new or renovated building, there will almost invariably be expenses associated with new staffing and technology. Particularly in a time of shrinking government resources, it may be difficult for criminal justice reformers to make the case that a community court is worthy of investment.

Strategies

While these obstacles shouldn't be minimized, they can be overcome if reformers are creative, flexible, and strategic. A few strategies in particular can help:

Performing Outreach

There is an enormous temptation to make quick work of the planning process in general, and community needs assessment in particular. This is a mistake. Fast tracking the creation of a community court to meet the schedules or demands of elected officials, funders, or other interested parties invariably creates as many problems as it solves.

It takes time to truly understand a neighborhood and its unique history, values, and cultural dynamics. For example, before launching the Red Hook Community Justice Center, our planning team met with scores of community groups, local residents, and neighborhood political leaders. These early meetings made it possible to hone our rationale for the project, ensure that proposed solutions actually matched local problems, and determine how to work productively with key stakeholders, both inside and outside the criminal justice system.

Over the course of many months, the Red Hook planning team built a base of supporters willing to donate resources, including community service supervision, social service staff time, and supplies. The early outreach also made it possible to recruit the court's community advisory board, which helps identify emerging problems in the neighborhood and potential community service projects. Just as important, we were able to find community voices who were willing to advocate for the project in the local press and to local elected officials—a key factor in the ultimate success of the project.

Winning Political and Financial Support

Even with the endorsement of local residents, a community court project won't get very far unless it enjoys enthusiastic support at the highest levels of local government. Community court planners can expect to invest significant time and energy explaining the idea and merits of the court to the leadership of the executive, legislative, and judicial branches.

Government must do more than endorse a community court, of course—it must provide resources (both manpower and money) to make the project happen. Fundraising efforts for the court should not be limited to traditional funders of criminal justice initiatives. Indeed, community court planners should take advantage of their project's capacity to make a visible difference in community life by appealing to local businesses, foundations, and nonprofit groups in addition to government funders.

Community courts have the potential to appeal to a wide variety of funders, including those interested in public health, housing, race relations, and at-risk youth. Organizations interested in economic development are another potential source of funding. After all, meaningful and lasting economic development rarely takes place in areas where residents, merchants, and employees fear for their safety. By addressing neighborhood blight, improving public safety, and providing social services, a community court can be a valuable addition to economic development efforts. Businesses, government agencies, and foundations with a stake in neighborhood economic development are a crucial constituency for community court planners. For example, the initial funding for the Harlem Community Justice Center came from the Upper Manhattan Empowerment Zone, a federally chartered effort to promote economic renewal in Harlem.

Creating Meaningful Alternative Sanctions

Communities won't be comfortable with community service, and judges and prosecutors won't utilize it, without some attention to risk and needs assessment. At Bronx Community Solutions, only misdemeanor offenders are sentenced to community service. Work projects are classified as high, medium, or low supervision. Each offender is matched to the appropriate level of supervision based on a review of his or her criminal history, background, and crime of arrest. At the Midtown Community Court, offenders with more extensive criminal histories and those considered less likely to complete their sentences are assigned to projects that take place in the courthouse (e.g., performing building maintenance, staffing a bulk mailing operation). Those considered lower risk are assigned to more visible outdoor projects (e.g., removing graffiti, painting fire hydrants and streetlights).

A community court's social service program will require similar attention; long-term drug treatment alone is not enough. In fact, inpatient drug treatment may not be an option in many cases. Since many low-level offenders face little or no jail time, the court must set up mandates that are proportional to the defendant's record and crime. Bronx Community Solutions has created an array of short-term interventions that take place in the courthouse itself, including a "treatment readiness" group that introduces defendants without serious records to drug treatment and prepares them for long-term help, group counseling sessions for prostitutes that offer basic health information and links to help for those who want to escape life on the streets, and job-readiness sessions that familiarize chronically unemployed defendants with job training programs.

While the immediate goals of these short-term interventions are modest, hundreds of defendants have used them as stepping stones toward changing their lives, and many voluntarily seek additional help after completing their sentence.

Staffing the Court

A community court requires a larger, more diverse staff than a traditional courthouse. In addition to clerks and security officers, community courts may need social workers, victim advocates, job developers, and managers for community service work projects, along with additional research and public information officers.

For example, Bronx Community Solutions has a full-time community outreach coordinator who is responsible for introducing the program to local merchants, community groups, and elected officials. The Harlem Community Justice Center has employed mediators to help resolve local conflicts. The Red Hook Community Justice Center has used technology specialists to help install a computerized data-sharing system.

These new staff do not necessarily need to be court employees. At the Midtown Community Court, several social service providers—both non-profit organizations and government agencies—have agreed to outsource personnel to the courthouse. The rationale is that service providers should bring resources to where the problem is, rather than vice versa. Every day the court interacts with dozens of people who are in need of the services that drug treatment providers, GED programs, and health care providers can deliver.

The Midtown Community Court also created a new role in the legal process: a resource coordinator, who is responsible for keeping track of all available sentencing options and helping the judge and attorneys match each defendant with the right program. The resource coordinator links criminal justice and social service professionals together. Situated in the courtroom, the resource coordinator is integrated into the case-processing system. At the same time, the coordinator is part of the court's clinical team, aware of treatment issues and the risks of success and failure. Over time, lawyers and judges have come to rely on resource coordinators and trust their recommendations.

Thinking Beyond the Courtroom

Many quality-of-life problems in a community are not violations of the law and do not come to the attention of the police or courts. There are various ways that community courts can address these problems.

The Red Hook Community Justice Center uses mediation to resolve neighborhood disputes (e.g., arguments between neighbors over noise) before they escalate to legal battles. In addition, the Justice Center actively seeks to convene local residents and government agencies to address problems that do not lend themselves to simple solutions. When local residents were having a problem with abandoned cars in an alley behind their homes, the Justice Center created a task force to deal with the problem. As a result, the Department of Sanitation agreed to tow away the cars and local residents agreed to improve lighting and signage to prevent the problem from happening again.

Abandoned cars are not a problem in Midtown Manhattan, but homelessness is. In response, the Midtown Community Court set up a street outreach unit to enroll potential clients in social service programs before they get into trouble with the law. The outreach team combed the neighborhood, engaging likely clients (e.g., prostitutes, substance abusers, the homeless) in conversation and encouraging them to come in for help voluntarily. The court has also worked to address homelessness by helping homeless individuals clear their outstanding warrants through engagement in services and by working with the city's Department of Homeless Services and Common Ground—a local supportive housing provider—to link homeless defendants to housing opportunities.

The Midtown Community Court also opened Times Square Ink, an on-the-job training program for ex-offenders who have "graduated" from community service. By providing ex-offenders—both those from the court and walk-ins from the street—with job training and help finding jobs, Times Square Ink seeks to address the related problems of unemployment and crime.

Conclusion

There is no magic recipe for creating a community court. While the experience of existing community courts offers a guide, planners in other jurisdictions will inevitably have to improvise to respond to unique conditions on the ground. The fact that there is no universal formula or 10-point-plan for community courts frustrates many people and probably has limited the prospects for replication. After all, there are other criminal justice innovations that are less complicated and labor-intensive. But for those who are willing to invest the time and energy, the potential rewards are significant: community courts have shown that they are capable of reducing local crime and disorder, improving perceptions of fairness, and bolstering public trust in government.

PART II

PROBLEM-SOLVING COURTS

4 Judicial Innovation in Action: The Rise of Problem-Solving Courts

Of all things I've written, this essay, which I co-authored with John Feinblatt under the title "Problem-Solving Courts: A Brief Primer" for Law & Policy in 2001, is probably the one that has generated the most sustained interest over time. Our goal in writing this piece was to cast a net over not just community courts but other contemporaneous developments such as drug courts, mental health courts, and domestic violence courts. This essay was one of the first attempts to define "problem-solving courts" as a collective. It is worth noting that in the years since John Feinblatt and I wrote this piece, numerous evaluations have been published that have further solidified our understanding of problem-solving courts and the positive impact they can have if implemented correctly. I have attempted to update the section on results to reflect some of this research. I also couldn't help changing a few sentences that I didn't like in the original.

Introduction

The past decades have been fertile ones for court reform. All across the country, courts—in concert with both government and community partners—have been experimenting with new ways to deliver justice. This wave of innovation goes by many names and takes many forms. Domestic violence court in Massachusetts. Drug court in Florida. Mental health court in Washington. Community court in New York. Each of these specialized courts targets different concerns in different places. And yet they all share a basic organizing theme—a desire to make courts more problem-solving and to improve results for victims, litigants, defendants and communities.

This essay is an attempt to identify several common elements that distinguish problem-solving courts from the way that cases are typically handled in today's state courts. Problem-solving courts use their authority to forge new responses to chronic social, human and legal problems—including problems like family dysfunction, addiction, delinquency and domestic violence—that have proven resistant to conventional solutions. They seek to broaden the focus of legal proceedings, from simply adjudicating past facts and legal issues to changing the future behavior of litigants and ensuring the well-being of communities. And they attempt to fix broken systems, making courts (and their partners) more accountable and responsive to their primary customers—the citizens who use courts every day.

The proliferation of problem-solving courts raises some important questions. Why now? What forces have sparked judges and attorneys across the country to innovate in this particular way? What results have problem-solving courts achieved? And what—if any—trade-offs have been made to accomplish these results?

This essay is an attempt to begin to answer these questions. It traces the history of problem-solving courts, outlines a basic set of problem-solving principles, and poses a set of questions that are worthy of further study as problem-solving courts move from experiment to institutionalization.

The Rise of Problem-Solving Courts

The recent wave of judicial experimentation in the United States began with the opening of the first "drug court" in Dade County, Florida in 1989. In an effort to address the problem of drug-fueled criminal recidivism, the Dade County court sentences addicted defendants to long-term, judicially-supervised drug treatment instead of incarceration. Participation in treatment is closely monitored by the drug court judge, who responds to progress or failure with a system of graduated rewards and sanctions, including short-term jail sentences. If a participant successfully completes treatment, the judge will reduce the charges or dismiss the case.

The results of the Dade County experiment have attracted national attention—and for good reason. A study by the National Institute of Justice revealed that Dade County drug court defendants had fewer re-arrests than comparable non-drug court defendants.[35] Based on these kinds of results, drug courts have become an increasingly standard feature of the judicial landscape across the country.[36]

Much of this activity (though by no means all) has been aided by federal funding decisions. In enacting the 1994 Crime Act, Congress authorized the Attorney General to make grants to establish drug courts across the country. The office charged with administering these grants at the U.S.

---

[35] National Institute of Justice. "Assessing the Impact of Dade County's Felony Drug Court: Executive Summary," *U.S. Department Of Justice* (1993).

[36] John Feinblatt, Greg Berman, Aubrey Fox. "Institutionalizing Innovation: The New York Drug Court Story," 28 *Fordham Urban Law Journal* 1 (October 2000), pp. 277-292.

Department of Justice distributed $50 million in fiscal year 2000—and has continued to allocate similar amounts each year since.

The wave of judicial innovation has not been confined to drugs. In the years since the opening of the Dade County drug court, dozens of other specialized, problem-solving courts have been developed to test new approaches to difficult cases and improve both case outcomes for parties and systemic outcomes for the community at large.[37] One example is the Midtown Community Court, which was launched in New York City in 1993. The Midtown Court targets misdemeanor "quality-of-life" crimes (prostitution, shoplifting, low-level drug possession, etc.) committed in and around Times Square. Low-level offenders are sentenced to perform community restitution—sweeping the streets, painting over graffiti, cleaning local parks—in an effort to "pay back" the community they have harmed through their criminal behavior.[38] The Court also mandates offenders to receive on-site social services, including health care, drug treatment and job training, in an effort to address the underlying problems that often lead to crime. At the same time, the Court has tested a variety of new mechanisms for engaging the local community in the criminal justice process, including advisory boards, community mediation, victim-offender impact panels, and town-hall meetings.

In Midtown's wake have come numerous replications. This progress has taken place in jurisdictions big and small, rich and poor. And it has been driven by a variety of different players, including judges, prosecutors, community advocates, and business leaders. As community courts have proliferated, so too have community court models. The next generation of community court innovators has not been content to simply replicate the Midtown Community Court. Rather, they have sought to push the model in new directions, including holding court sessions at local community centers and targeting problems related to neglected and abandoned properties. As with drug courts, the U.S. Department of Justice has played a key role in community court replication. Although there has been no dedicated funding stream for community courts, the Justice Department has provided technical assistance and advice to jurisdictions interested in the model.

Similar stories can be told about the birth and expansion of domestic violence courts, mental health courts and others: an initial innovation seeks to address a recurring problem within the courts, attracts the attention of the press, elected officials and funders, and is quickly followed by a wave of replications.

---

[37] John Feinblatt, Greg Berman, Derek Denckla. "Judicial Innovation at the Crossroads: The Future of Problem Solving Courts," 15 *Court Manager* 28 (2000).

[38] John Feinblatt, Greg Berman, Michele Sviridoff. "Neighborhood Justice at the Midtown Community Court," *Crime and Place: Plenary Papers of the 1997 Conference on Criminal Justice Research and Evaluation*, National Institute of Justice (1998).

Why Now?

What's going on here? Why are judges, attorneys and court administrators all over the country experimenting with new ways of doing business? A number of social and historical forces have helped set the stage for problem-solving innovation. This includes a breakdown among many social and community institutions that have traditionally addressed problems like addiction, mental illness, and domestic violence. At the same time, a surge in the nation's incarcerated population, and the resulting prison overcrowding, has forced many policymakers to re-think their approaches to crime. Another important factor is the reality that the quality and availability of therapeutic interventions have advanced significantly in recent years, giving criminal justice practitioners greater confidence in using certain forms of treatment (particularly drug treatment) in attempts to address defendants' underlying problems.

But perhaps the most important forces that have contributed to the development of problem-solving courts are rising caseloads and increasing frustration—both among the public and among system players—with the standard approach to case processing and case outcomes in state courts.

In recent years, many state court systems have been inundated with growing caseloads. And in the eyes of many judges, attorneys and court administrators, much of this growth has been driven by the intersection of social, human, and legal problems, including domestic violence, addiction, and chronic low-level offending. From 1984 to 1997, for example, the number of domestic violence cases in state courts increased by seventy-seven percent.[39] National research also suggests that as many as three out of every four defendants in major cities test positive for drugs at the time of arrest.[40] Many jurisdictions have also experienced an explosion in quality-of-life crime. In New York City, for example, over the past decade the number of misdemeanor cases has increased by eighty-five percent.[41]

The sheer volume of cases has placed enormous pressure on judges and attorneys to process cases as quickly as possible, with little regard to the problems of victims, communities or defendants. This has led many—victims, police officers, journalists, and even judges and attorneys—to conclude that many front-line state courts are practicing "revolving door" justice. As former New York State Chief Judge Judith S. Kaye has written:

---

[39] David Rottman and Pamela Casey. "Therapeutic Jurisprudence and the Emergence of Problem-Solving Courts," *National Institute of Justice Journal* (July 1999), p. 18.

[40] National Institute of Justice. "Assessing the Impact of Dade County's Felony Drug Court: Executive Summary," *U.S. Department of Justice* (1998).

[41] Greg Rohde. "Crackdown on Minor Offenses Swamps New York City Courts," *The New York Times*, February 2, 1999.

In many of today's cases, the traditional approach yields unsatisfying results. The addict arrested for drug dealing is adjudicated, does time, then goes right back to dealing on the street. The battered wife obtains a protective order, goes home and is beaten again. Every legal right of the litigants is protected, all procedures followed, yet we aren't making a dent in the underlying problem. Not good for the parties involved. Not good for the community. Not good for the courts.[42]

Kaye is hardly alone in her analysis; a sense of growing frustration with "business as usual" in the state courts can be felt among the public, judges and attorneys.

Public frustration gets expressed in many ways, most notably in declining confidence in the criminal justice system (and those who work within it) and increasing fear of crime (even as crime rates across the country fall). Michael Schrunk, who served for many years as the elected district attorney in Portland, Oregon, has said that his endorsement of problem-solving courts grows out of a concern about the gaps between communities and the justice system. According to Schrunk, "It's all well and good for us to read about the Microsoft trial or the O.J. Simpson trial, but that's a very, very small percentage of what goes on in the world of our constituents. I strongly believe we've got to work on public credibility, because a lot of citizens, quite frankly, they don't think judges are relevant."[43]

Many state court judges have reported that the pressure of processing hundreds of cases each day has transformed their courtrooms into "plea bargain mills," which place the highest value on disposing of the maximum number of cases in the minimum amount of time.[44] Additionally, they bemoan their lack of tools—both information and sentencing options—for responding to the complexities of drug addiction, mental illness and domestic violence cases. Kathleen Blatz, formerly the chief justice of Minnesota, neatly summarized the feelings of many judges: "Judges are very frustrated.... The innovation that we're seeing now is a result of judges processing cases like a vegetable factory. Instead of cans of peas, you've got cases. You just move 'em, move 'em, move 'em. One of my colleagues on the bench said, 'You know, I feel like I work for McJustice: we sure aren't good for you, but we are fast.'"[45]

In recent years, many attorneys have begun to take a closer look at the roles they play and the outcomes they achieve. In addition to problem-solving courts, this examination has led some to advocate for new forms

---

[42] Judith S. Kaye. "Making the Case for Hands-On Courts," *Newsweek,* October 11, 1999, p. 13.

[43] Greg Berman, ed. "What Is A Traditional Judge Anyway?: Problem Solving in the State Courts," 84 *Judicature* 2 (2000).

[44] Judith S. Kaye. "Making the Case for Hands-On Courts,"*Newsweek,* October 11, 1999, p. 13.

[45] Greg Berman, ed. "What Is A Traditional Judge Anyway?: Problem Solving in the State Courts," 84 *Judicature* 2 (2000).

of lawyering, including calls for "therapeutic jurisprudence," "public safety lawyering," and "client-centered counseling."[46] What all of these new approaches share is an understanding that lawyers need to employ new sets of tools—in many cases outside of the traditional adversarial model—to effectively represent the interests of their clients. According to Patrick McGrath, deputy district attorney in San Diego, California, "I think it's fair to say there's a sense of yearning out there [among attorneys]. If you grab a judge, a defense attorney and prosecutor and sat them down together and bought them a round of drinks ... they'll all complain about the same thing: 'I have all of this education and what do I do? I work on an assembly line. I don't affect case outcomes.'"[47] While the yearning for a new way of thinking about advocacy is far from universal—there are still, after all, plenty of practitioners of win-at-all-costs advocacy—the voices of reform are now plentiful and strong enough that they can no longer be easily dismissed.

Both internal and external critics of state courts have cited a number of examples to underline their concerns with the standard approach to case processing. For instance, they have pointed to low-level criminal cases, where many offenders walk away from court without receiving any sanctions. Researchers found that prior to the opening of the Midtown Community Court in New York, four out of every ten misdemeanor offenders walked out of court without receiving either a meaningful punishment or any kind of help for their underlying problems. Outcomes in domestic violence cases are equally problematic. High probation violation rates are one sign that court mandates are not deterring continued violence.[48] One study showed that thirty-four percent of batterers violated orders of protection.[49] Nor is the problem of recidivism confined to domestic violence—it is estimated that over fifty percent of offenders convicted of drug possession will recidivate within two or three years.[50]

In short, advocates of problem-solving justice have argued that state courts find it difficult to address the underlying problems of individual litigants, the social problems of communities or the structural and operational problems of a fractured justice system. As Ellen Schall of New York University's Wagner Graduate School of Public Service has noted, "I think we have

---

[46]   David B. Wexler, "Two Decades of Therapeutic Jurisprudence," 24 *Touro Law Review* 1 (1998), pp. 17-29.

[47]   John Feinblatt and Derek Denckla. "What Does It Mean To Be A Good Lawyer?: Prosecutors and Defenders in Problem-Solving Courts," 84 Judicature 4 (2001), p. 209.

[48]   Betsy Tsai. "The Trend Towards Specialized Domestic Violence Courts: Improvements on an Effective Innovation," 68 *Fordham Law Review* (2000), p. 1285.

[49]   Brian Ostrom and Neal Kauder, eds. *A National Perspective from the Court Statistics Project*, National Center for State Courts (1998).

[50]   Office of Justice Programs, Drug Court Clearinghouse and Technical Assistance Project, "Looking at a Decade of Drug Courts," *American University* (1999), p. 6.

to begin from the notion that the system from which the problem-solving courts have emerged was a failure on any count. It wasn't a legal success. It wasn't a social success. It wasn't working."[51]

What is a Problem-Solving Court?

Problem-solving courts are a response to the frustrations engendered by overwhelmed state courts that struggle to address the problems that are fueling their rising caseloads. They are an attempt to achieve better outcomes while at the same time protecting individual rights. While drug courts, community courts, domestic violence courts, mental health courts and other problem-solving initiatives address different problems, they do share some common elements:

Case Outcomes. Problem-solving courts seek to achieve tangible outcomes for victims, for offenders and for society. These include reductions in recidivism, reduced stays in foster care for children, increased sobriety for addicts and healthier communities. As former New York State Chief Judge Judith Kaye has written, "outcomes—not just process and precedents—matter. Protecting the rights of an addicted mother is important. So is protecting her children and getting her off drugs."[52]

System Change. In addition to re-examining individual case outcomes, problem-solving courts also seek to re-engineer how government systems respond to problems like addiction, mental illness and child neglect. This means promoting reform outside of the courthouse as well as within. For example, family treatment courts that handle cases of child neglect have encouraged local child welfare agencies to adopt new staffing patterns and to improve case management practices.

Judicial Authority. Problem-solving courts rely upon the active use of judicial authority to solve problems and to change the behavior of litigants. Instead of passing off cases—to other judges, to probation departments, to community-based treatment programs—judges at problem-solving courts stay involved with each case throughout the post-adjudication process. Drug court judges, for example, closely supervise the performance of offenders in drug treatment, requiring them to return to court frequently for urine testing and courtroom progress reports.

Collaboration. Problem-solving courts employ a collaborative approach, relying on both government and non-profit partners (criminal justice agencies, social service providers, community groups and others) to help achieve their goals. For example, many domestic violence courts have

---

[51] Greg Berman, ed. "What Is A Traditional Judge Anyway?: Problem Solving in the State Courts," 84 *Judicature* 2 (2000).

[52] Judith S. Kaye. "Making the Case for Hands-On Courts," *Newsweek,* October 11, 1999, p. 13.

developed partnerships with batterers' programs and probation departments to help improve the monitoring of defendants.

Non-Traditional Roles. Some problem-solving courts have altered the dynamics of the courtroom, including, at times, certain features of the adversarial process. For example at many drug courts, judges and attorneys (on both sides of the aisle) work together to craft systems of sanctions and rewards for offenders in drug treatment. And by using the institution's authority and prestige to coordinate the work of other agencies, problem-solving courts may engage judges in unfamiliar roles as conveners and brokers.

The cumulative impact of these changes has been significant, and not just on the judges and lawyers who staff problem-solving courts. Problemsolving courts are still relatively new, but there are signs that they have begun to have a tangible impact on thousands of victims, defendants and community residents. This includes domestic violence victims who have been linked to safe shelter, residents of high-crime areas who no longer have to avoid local parks at night, formerly-addicted mothers who have been reunited with their children, and mentally-ill defendants who have received meaningful treatment for the first time.

Results

How much is known about the results of problem-solving courts?[53] As the most well-established brand of problem-solving court, drug courts have the longest track record. The evidence shows that drug courts have achieved solid results with regard to reducing drug use and recidivism and saving jail and prison costs.

In a meta-analysis published in 2012 of more than 150 drug courts, both adult and DUI drug courts were found to produce significant reductions in criminal re-offending.[54] Although most evaluations tracked defendants over two years or less, several studies of adult drug courts extended the follow-up period to three years or longer and still reported positive effects.[55]

Besides reducing recidivism, research also suggests that adult drug

---

[53] Thanks to Michael Rempel, the director of research at the Center for Court Innovation, for his help revising this section.

[54] Ojmarrh Mitchell, David B. Wilson, Amy Eggers, and Doris L. MacKenzie. "Assessing the Effectiveness of Drug Courts on Recidivism: A Meta-Analytic Review of Traditional and Non-Traditional Drug Courts," 40 *Journal of Criminal Justice* (2012), pp. 60-71.

[55] For example, see Denise C. Gottfredson, Brook W. Kearley, Stacy S. Najaka, and Carlos M. Rocha. "Long-term Effects of Participation in the Baltimore City Drug Treatment Court: Results from an Experimental Study," 2 *Journal of Experimental Criminology* 1 (2006), pp. 67-98; Michael W. Finigan, Shannon M. Carey, and Anton Cox. "The Impact of a Mature Drug Court Over 10 Years of Operation: Recidivism and Costs," *NPC Research* (2007); Michael Rempel, Dana Fox-Kralstein, Amanda Cissner, Robyn Cohen, Melissa Labriola, Donald Farole, Ann Bader, and Michael Magnani. "The New York State Adult Drug Court Evaluation: Policies, Participants, and Impacts," *Center for Court Innovation* (2003).

courts reduce the drug use and dependency problems that give rise to criminal behavior in the first place. The National Institute of Justice's *Multi-Site Adult Drug Court Evaluation*, a study of 23 adult drug courts from around the country, found that they significantly reduced drug use over an 18-month tracking period, echoing the findings of several previous studies that directly measured drug use at follow-up.[56]

In addition to these impacts on participants, a growing body of research suggests that adult drug courts produce significant cost savings. In general, incarceration is far more costly than either residential or outpatient treatment, and reducing recidivism produces tremendous savings to individuals who would otherwise have been victimized by crimes that drug courts prevented from happening. A statewide evaluation of California's adult drug courts found that eight of nine sites produced savings for taxpayers at an average of $5,139 per participant.[57] The National Institute of Justice's *Multi-Site Adult Drug Court Evaluation* reported similar average savings of $5,680 per participant across 23 sites, with the greatest savings accruing to individuals who, in the absence of drug courts, would otherwise have been victimized by recidivist violent or property crimes.[58]

Research to date makes clear that the success of the adult model has not been equaled by juvenile drug courts. A recent meta-analysis of 34 juvenile drug court evaluations detected mixed results from site to site, although the average program still produced a modest reduction in recidivism.[59] Some researchers have found, however, that when juvenile drug courts employ certain key practices, they become truly effective. Specifically, juvenile drug courts produce more positive outcomes when they facilitate pro-social activities with peers, limit contact with demonstrably anti-social peers, involve family members in judicial status hearings, and employ evidence-based treatments such as Multi-Systemic Therapy.[60]

---

[56] Shelli B. Rossman, John K. Roman, Janine M. Zweig, Michael Rempel, and Christine H. Lindquist, eds. *The Multi-Site Adult Drug Court Evaluation.* Urban Institute (2011). And see also, Denise C. Gottfredson, Brook W. Kearley, Stacy S. Najaka, and Carlos M. Rocha. "The Baltimore City Drug Treatment Court: 3-year outcome study," 29 *Evaluation Review* 1 (2005), pp. 42-64; Adele Harrell, John Roman, and Emily Sack. "Drug Court Services for Female Offenders, 1996-1999: Evaluation of the Brooklyn Treatment Court," *Urban Institute* (2001).

[57] Shannon M. Carey, David Crumpton, Michael W. Finigan and Mark S. Waller. "California Drug Courts: A Methodology for Determining Costs and Benefits, Phase II: Testing the Methodology: Final Report," *NPC Research* (2005).

[58] Rossman et al. *The Multi-Site Drug Court Evaluation.*

[59] Mitchell et al. "Assessing the Effectiveness of Drug Courts on Recidivism."

[60] See Christopher Salvatore, Jaime S. Henderson, Matthew L. Hiller et al. "An Observational Study of Team Meetings and Status Hearings in a Juvenile Drug Court," 7 *Drug Court Review* 1 (2010), pp. 95-124; Cindy M. Schaeffer, Scott W. Henggeler, Jason E. Chapman et al. "Mechanisms of effectiveness in Juvenile Drug Court: Altering Risk Processes Associated with Delinquency and Substance Abuse," 7 *Drug Court Review* 1 (2010), pp. 57-94.

Family drug courts, which seek both to reduce substance abuse by the respondent parent and to achieve a positive permanency outcome for the child, have also generated some positive results. Across several family drug courts that have been evaluated, five of seven produced increased treatment completion rates for the respondent; and six of eight produced increased rates of parent-child reunification than equivalent comparison groups.[61]

Less is known about the impacts of mental health courts, domestic violence courts, and community courts. However, over the past decade a small but growing body of rigorous evaluations has emerged on these newer problem-solving models.

Although only a handful of rigorous studies have been performed on mental health courts, since the principles and practices applied by these courts are analogous to adult drug courts, it is logical to expect that the results would be similar. Indeed, two recent evaluations examining a total of six mental health courts, spread across four different states, found that they reduced recidivism as well as incarceration for participating defendants.[62]

Across eleven rigorous evaluations, some domestic violence courts have been shown to reduce recidivism, but others have not.[63] In taking a closer look at this literature, it appears that domestic violence courts may produce greater recidivism reductions with *convicted* offenders, over whom the court has more leverage to order program participation, judicial monitoring, or intensive probation monitoring than with offenders whose cases end in dismissal.[64] It also appears that domestic violence courts like those in Dorchester, Massachusetts and Milwaukee, Wisconsin, which make consistent use of probation revocations and other sanctions in response to noncompliance with court orders, are especially successful at reducing recidivism.[65]

---

[61] See original studies and reviews of other family drug court studies in Sarah Fritsche, Jennifer Bryan, Dana Kralstein, and Erin Farley. "The Bronx Family Treatment Court 2005-2010: Impact on family court outcomes and participant experiences and perceptions," *Center for Court Innovation* (2011); Beth L. Green, Carrie J. Furrer, Sonia D. Worcel et al. "Building the Evidence Base for Family Drug Treatment Courts: Results from Recent Outcome Studies," 6 *Drug Court Review* 2 (2009), pp. 53-82.

[62] Henry J. Steadman, Allison Redlich, Lisa Callahan et al. "Effect of Mental Health Courts on Arrests and Jail Days: A Multisite Study," 68 *Archives of General Psychiatry* 2 (2010), pp. 167-172; Shelli B. Rossman, Janeen Buck Willison, Kamala Mallik-Kane et al. "Criminal Justice Interventions for Offenders with Mental Illness: Evaluation of Mental Health Courts in Bronx and Brooklyn, New York." *Urban Institute* (2011).

[63] See original study and literature reviewed in Amanda B. Cissner, Melissa M. Labriola, and Michael Rempel. "Testing the Effects of New York's Domestic Violence Courts," *Center for Court Innovation* (2012).

[64] Amanda B. Cissner et al. "Testing the Effects of New York's Domestic Violence Courts."

[65] See, also, Christy A. Visher, Adele Harrell, Lisa Newmark, and Jennifer Yahner. "Reducing Intimate Partner Violence: An Evaluation of a Comprehensive Justice System Community Collaboration," 7 *Criminology and Public Policy* 4 (2008), pp. 495-523.

Importantly, not all domestic violence court practitioners seek to achieve recidivism reductions as a primary goal. Many of these courts prioritize, instead, the goals of holding offenders accountable for their violent behavior (through increased conviction rates and increased use of sanctions for noncompliance with court orders) and of providing safety planning and other services for victims.[66] In these regards, research to date suggests that domestic violence courts have been generally successful.[67]

Community courts are in many ways unique among problem-solving models, because they seek to address the multiple sources of crime in a community rather than a single "problem" (such as drug addiction, mental illness, or domestic violence). The most detailed evaluations of a community court are the National Center for State Courts's assessments of the Midtown Community Court and the Red Hook Community Justice Center. The National Center's team of researchers found that the Midtown Court had helped reduce low-level crime in the neighborhood: prostitution arrests dropped sixty-three percent and illegal vending dropped twenty-four percent.[68] Supervised offenders performing community service contributed more than $175,000 worth of labor to the local community each year.[69]

Just as important, findings from a telephone survey of 500 area residents suggest that the Midtown experiment made an impression in the court of public opinion. Sixty-four percent of the respondents said that they were willing to pay additional taxes for a community court.[70] And according to evaluators, these results have been achieved without sacrificing efficiency. In fact, by keeping defendants and police officers in the neighborhood instead of transporting them to the downtown courthouse, the Midtown Court cut the time between arrest and arraignment in 1994 by forty-five percent.[71]

The Red Hook evaluation documented reductions in re-offending among both juvenile and adult participants at the Justice Center as well

---

[66]   Melissa Labriola, Sarah Bradley, Chris S. O'Sullivan, Michael Rempel, and Samantha Moore. "National Portrait of Domestic Violence Courts," *Center for Court Innovation* (2009).

[67]   See Amanda B. Cissner et al. "Testing the Effects of New York's Domestic Violence Courts"; Visher et al. "Reducing Intimate Partner Violence"; Lisa Newmark, Michael Rempel, Kelly Diffily, and Kamala Malik Kane. "Specialized Felony Domestic Violence Courts: Lessons on Implementation and Impacts from the Kings County Experience," *Urban Institute* (2001).

[68]   Richard Curtis et al. *Dispensing Justice Locally: The Implementation and Effects of the Midtown Community Court,* Harwood Academic Publishers, 2000, p. 155.

[69]   John Feinblatt and Greg Berman. "Responding to the Community: Principles for Planning and Creating a Community Court," *U.S. Department of Justice* (February 2001), p. 2.

[70]   Richard Curtis et al. "Dispensing Justice Locally: The Impact, Costs and Benefits of the Midtown Community Court," *National Criminal Justice Reference Service* (September 2002), pp. 7-13.

[71]   Curtis et al. *Dispensing Justice Locally,* p. 203.

as significant changes in sentencing practice. By increasing the availability of alternative sanctions, the Justice Center reduced the number of defendants who received jail sentences. Researchers also documented sustained reductions in misdemeanor arrest rates in Red Hook's local precinct. And an ethnographic research team found that participants at the Justice Center expressed high rates of satisfaction with the Justice Center and its procedures—evidence that the Justice Center may have improved perceptions of the legitimacy of the justice system.

Tensions

The results of problem-solving courts have earned these projects high marks from many elected officials, reporters, and funders. They have also fueled the field's rapid expansion. Good results do not insulate problem-solving courts from scrutiny, however. After all, problem-solving reforms are happening within a branch of government that is understandably cautious about innovation. Core judicial values—certainty, reliability, impartiality and fairness—have been safeguarded over many generations largely through a reliance on tradition and precedent. As a result, efforts to introduce new ways of doing justice are always subjected to careful scrutiny.

Problem-solving courts are no exception to this rule, nor should they be. Critics have questioned both their results[72] and their ability to preserve the individual rights of defendants.[73] While the academic literature on problem-solving courts is still emerging, it seems clear that there are a number of areas of potential tension between this new brand of jurisprudence and standard practice in state courts:

Coercion. What procedures exist to ensure that a defendant's consent to participate in a problem-solving court is fairly and freely given? Are problem-solving courts any more coercive than the current practice of plea bargaining that resolves the large majority of criminal cases in this country?

Zealous Advocacy. Is advocacy in a problem-solving court more or less zealous than in a traditional court? Does problem-solving demand new definitions of effective lawyering? How should attorneys measure their effectiveness—by the case or by the person? To what extent do problem-solving courts actually help attorneys—both prosecutors and defenders—realize their professional goals?

Structure. Do problem-solving courts give greater license to judges to make rulings based on their own idiosyncratic world views rather than the law? Or, with their predetermined schemes of graduated sanctions and re-

---

[72] Morris B. Hoffman. "The Drug Court Scandal," 78 *North Carolina Law Review* (June 2000), pp. 1437-1534.

[73] Carl Baar. "The Role of the Courts: Two Faces of Justice," presented at the *Third National Symposium on Court Management* Atlanta, Georgia, August 13-18, 2000.

wards, do problem-solving courts actually limit the discretion of judges and provide more uniform justice than traditional courts?

Impartiality. As judges become better informed about specialized classes of cases, is their impartiality affected? As they solicit the wisdom of social scientists, researchers and clinicians, are they more likely to become engaged in ex parte communication?

Paternalism. Are problem-solving judges imposing treatment regimes on defendants without reference to the complexity of individuals' problems? Do problem-solving courts widen the net of governmental control? Or are they simply an effort by judges and attorneys to deal more constructively and humanely with the underlying problems of the people who come to court?

Separation of Powers. Do problem-solving courts inappropriately blur the lines between the branches of government? As judges become involved in activities like convening, brokering and organizing, are they infringing upon the territory of the executive branch? Are they, in effect, making policy? Or are judges simply taking advantage of the discretion they have traditionally been afforded over sentencing to craft more meaningful sanctions?

There are several important realities to keep in mind as one attempts to make sense of these tensions. The first is context. When weighing the merits of any reform effort, it is always important to ask the question: compared to what? Proponents of problem-solving courts have been adamant about not allowing critics to pick apart these new initiatives by comparing them to an idealized vision of justice that does not exist in real life. They point to the fact that the large majority of criminal, housing and family court cases today are handled in courts that Roscoe Pound and John Marshall would scarcely recognize. Judge Judy Harris Kluger, an administrator in New York, has described standard practice in the state courts this way: "For a long time, my claim to fame was that I arraigned two hundred cases in one session. That's ridiculous. When I was arraigning cases, I'd be handed the papers, say the sentence is going to be five days, ten days, whatever, never even looking at the defendant."[74] Under these circumstances, it is fair to question the extent to which many frontline state courts measure up to their own ideals of doing justice. While the excesses of today's "McJustice" courts do not justify any and all reform efforts, they do help explain why so many judges and attorneys have been attracted to new ways of doing business. And they do provide a valuable context for evaluating the merits of problem-solving courts.

In addition, any effort to separate the wheat from the chaff with problem-solving courts must take into account what might be called the "shoddy practice effect." Put simply, some of the concerns raised by critics of

---

[74] Greg Berman, ed. "What Is A Traditional Judge Anyway?: Problem Solving in the State Courts," 84 *Judicature* 2 (2000).

problem-solving courts are a response to the failings of individual judges, attorneys, and courtrooms rather than an indictment of anything intrinsic to problem-solving courts. These issues include courts that have been created without any consultation with the local defense bar; courts that have failed to offer specialized training to the attorneys that work within them; courts in which defendants are not given a meaningful opportunity to raise factual and Fourth Amendment defenses; courts in which "back-up" incarceration sentences for defendants who fail to comply are out of proportion to the sanctions that the defendant would have originally faced; and courts that have done little to ensure that social service interventions are effective and culturally appropriate.

While serious, these are all issues that might reasonably be resolved by better planning and the development and dissemination of best practices. In fact, there are already signs that problem-solving innovators in the field are beginning to adapt their models to address these issues. For example, problem-solving courts in Seattle and Portland have instituted structures that give defendants several weeks to test out treatment while their case is still pending. Defendants can use this period to decide whether to opt into or out of the program, while their defense attorneys can use the time to investigate the strength of the case against their client.[75]

Fairness

Not all questions about problem-solving courts can be explained away by bad practice or the widespread problems of today's mill courts, however. The most pointed critiques have asked whether problem-solving courts' emphasis on improving case outcomes and protecting public order has come at the expense of the rights of defendants.[76] Are problem-solving courts fair? Have they fundamentally altered the rights protections typically found in today's criminal courts? Courts have traditionally relied on zealous advocacy as a bulwark against these kinds of concerns, so the role of attorneys at problem-solving courts is an issue that merits special scrutiny.[77] Michael Smith of the University of Wisconsin Law School has been particularly vocal in articulating the importance of advocates to problem-solving courts: "One of the things that judges and courts are particularly useful at when they're not just milling people is fact-finding. But a fact-finding court is heavily reliant on advocates if it's any good.... If we don't figure out a way to take

---

[75] John Feinblatt and Derek Denckla. "What Does It Mean To Be A Good Lawyer?: Prosecutors and Defenders in Problem-Solving Courts," 84 *Judicature* 4 (2001), pp. 206-214.

[76] Carl Baar. The Role of the Courts: Two Faces of Justice," presented at the *Third National Symposium on Court Management* Atlanta, Georgia, August 13-18, 2000.

[77] John Feinblatt, Greg Berman, Derek Denckla. "Judicial Innovation at the Crossroads: The Future of Problem Solving Courts," 15 *Court Manager* 28 (2000).

advantage of that, then we're not going to have very good problem-solving courts. The courts will be no better than the social service clinics, which have failed to address these problems. So the adversary system and the presence of defense counsel are of enormous value in problem-solving."[78]

The nature of advocacy in problem-solving courts is the subject of some debate. Some look at the "team approach" of drug courts, where all of the courtroom players work together to support defendant's participation in treatment, and declare that defense attorneys have abdicated their role as forceful advocates on behalf of their clients. Others argue that adversarialism is alive and well in problem-solving courts. They point to the fact that throughout the adjudication process—up until a defendant decides, by virtue of pleading to reduced charges, to enter treatment—prosecutors and defenders in problem-solving courts typically relate to one another as they always have: as adversaries. In addition to contesting the merits of each case, advocates in drug courts also argue about eligibility criteria, the length of treatment sentences and appropriate treatment modalities.[79]

In general, what's different about problem-solving courts are the activities that take place after adjudication, as judges and attorneys become engaged in the ongoing monitoring of defendants instead of leaving this job to probation departments or community-based organizations (or, in all too many cases, to no one at all).[80] As the late John Goldkamp of Temple University observed, "Generally, adversarial procedures are employed at the screening and admission stage and at the conclusion of drug court, when participants are terminated and face legal consequences or graduate. During the drug court process, however, formal adversarial rules generally do not apply."[81] As Goldkamp's formulation makes plain, by and large, problem-solving courts seem to emphasize traditional due process protections during the adjudication phase of a case and the achievement of tangible, constructive outcomes post-adjudication. In doing so, problem-solving courts have sought to balance fairness and effectiveness, the protection of individual rights and the preservation of public order.[82]

---

[78] Greg Berman, ed. "What Is A Traditional Judge Anyway?: Problem Solving in the State Courts," 84 *Judicature* 2 (2000).

[79] Feinblatt et al. "Judicial Innovation at the Crossroads."

[80] It is worth noting that some drug courts and community courts—and many domestic violence courts—depart from the standard problem-solving model, mandating defendants to pretrial rather than post-disposition interventions. These courts may raise additional questions from those concerned with due process protections.

[81] John S. Goldkamp. "The Drug Court Response: Issues and Implications for Justice Change," 63 *Albany Law Review* (2000), p. 952.

[82] John Feinblatt, Greg Berman, Derek Denckla. "Judicial Innovation at the Crossroads: The Future of Problem Solving Courts," 15 *Court Manager* 28 (2000).

To what extent have problem-solving courts achieved this delicate balancing act? It varies from jurisdiction to jurisdiction. And it depends upon the perspective of the person asking the question. Conversations about the fairness of problem-solving courts often spark a Rashomon effect, with judges having one response, prosecutors another and defenders yet a third.[83]

There is little doubt that the tensions between problem-solving courts and conventional state courts are felt particularly acutely by defenders. There is an almost palpable sense of ambivalence on the part of many defenders towards problem-solving courts. After all, defense attorneys have been arguing for years that courts should make more aggressive use of drug treatment, mental health counseling and other alternative sanctions. Problem-solving courts have begun to deliver on this expectation, but at the cost of greater state involvement in the lives of some of their clients. Are there any historical antecedents that might guide defenders as they wrestle with competing professional demands? What are their ethical obligations to their clients, given the changing judicial landscape? Is there a need for new standards of effective lawyering at problem-solving courts? These are issues that merit deeper investigation and additional scholarship.

Conclusion

Now is an important moment to begin to look at the questions raised by problem-solving courts. Problem-solving courts have achieved a kind of critical mass. They are no longer just a set of isolated experiments driven by entrepreneurial judges and administrators. According to John Goldkamp, "What we have now is not a bunch of little hobbies that judges have in isolated jurisdictions, but rather a paradigm shift that larger court systems are trying to come to grips with. They're at your door step. The question isn't: Gosh, are courts supposed to be doing this? It's: What are you going to do about it? How does it fit in? It's no longer a question of whether this should have been invented. They're here."[84]

Problem-solving courts have begun to spark the interest of not just front-line practitioners, but the chief judges and administrators who make decisions about court policies and court operations. The signs are unmistakable. Problem-solving courts continue to multiply. California and New York are overhauling the way that their courts handle drug cases. And the Conference of Chief Justices and the Conference of State Court Administrators has passed a joint resolution that pledges to "encourage the broad

---

[83] John Feinblatt and Derek Denckla. "What Does It Mean To Be A Good Lawyer?: Prosecutors and Defenders in Problem-Solving Courts," 84 *Judicature* 4 (2001).

[84] Greg Berman, ed. "What Is A Traditional Judge Anyway?: Problem Solving in the State Courts," 84 *Judicature* 2 (2000).

integration, over the next decade, of the principles and methods employed in problem solving courts into the administration of justice."[85]

Formal institutionalization of any new idea does not come easy, however. If problem-solving courts are to accomplish this goal—if they truly hope to infiltrate the mainstream of thinking about law and justice in this country—they must begin to preach to the unconverted. This means reaching out to the skeptics and the uninitiated within state courts—defenders concerned about due process protections, administrators worried about the allocation of limited resources, and prosecutors and judges who see nothing wrong with the way they've been doing their jobs for years.

And it means reaching outside of the system as well—to law schools and bar associations and elected officials. In the process, advocates of problem-solving courts must tackle some of the policy and procedural concerns that have been outlined in this essay. And they must begin to think through the problems of going to scale, of how small-scale experiments can be translated into system-wide reform.

These are not insignificant challenges, to be sure. But given the tangible results that the first generation of problem-solving courts have achieved— reduced recidivism among drug-addicted and mentally-ill offenders, reduced probation violation and dismissal rates in domestic violence cases, and improved public safety (and confidence in justice) in communities harmed by crime—they are challenges well worth pursuing.

---

[85] Conference of Chief Justices, Conference of State Court Administrators. "In Support of Problem-Solving Courts," CCJ Resolution 22/COSCA Resolution IV (August 2000).

5

A Paradigm Shift: Problem-Solving Justice and Traditional Practice in the Courts

One of my favorite projects at the Center for Court Innovation has been helping to put together roundtables devoted to controversial topics of justice reform. This is an edited transcript from our first such gathering, which explored the challenges that problem-solving courts present to state courts. It was great fun to whittle the conversation down to a manageable length for inclusion in Judicature under the title "What Is A Traditional Judge Anyway?" (Volume 84, Issue No. 2, 2000). It appears here without revision. All participants in the conversation are listed according to their position and affiliation at the time of the roundtable. One of the leading voices on the day was John Goldkamp, a professor at Temple University who has since passed away. John's spirit of pragmatism and his commitment to improving the justice system had an impact on me during a formative stage of my career. I hope traces of these values can be seen in this, and other, chapters of this book.

Introduction

Over the past decade, problem-solving courts have generated healthy debate among both proponents and critics. Advocates of problem-solving courts hail improved case outcomes, including reductions in crime, increased sobriety for addicts, safer neighborhoods, fewer probation violations, and enhanced public confidence in justice. Skeptics question whether the new courts are engaged in practices—including monitoring defendants in treatment, listening to community concerns, and forging collaborations with government and non-profit agencies to solve discrete problems—that are inconsistent with the traditional values of the judicial branch. In late 1999, a select group of judges, attorneys, policy makers, and scholars were convened by the Office of Justice Programs, U.S. Department of Justice, the Open Society Institute (Program in Law and Society), and the Center for

Court Innovation. What follows is an edited transcript of the conversation, which took place over the course of six hours in a Washington D.C. conference room.

Participants

Kathleen Blatz, Chief Justice, Supreme Court of Minnesota

Richard Cappalli, Klein Chair in Law and Government, Temple Law School

James Cayce, Presiding Judge, King County, Washington, District Court

Kathleen Clark, Professor, Washington University School of Law

Cait Clarke, Lecturer, Harvard University, Kennedy School of Government

Legrome Davis, Supervising Judge, Criminal Division, Court of Common Pleas, Philadelphia

John Goldkamp, Professor of Criminal Justice, Temple University

Judith S. Kaye, Chief Judge, New York State Court of Appeals

Judy Harris Kluger, Administrative Judge, New York City Criminal Court

Eric Lane, Eric J. Schmertz Professor of Public Law and Public Service, Hofstra Law School (Moderator)

Cindy Lederman, Administrative Judge, Juvenile Division, 11th Judicial Circuit, Florida

Candace McCoy, Professor, Rutgers University School of Criminal Justice

Truman Morrison, III, Judge, District of Columbia Superior Court

William Nelson, Joel and Anne Ehrenkranz Professor of Law, New York University Law School

Ellen Schall, Martin Cherkasky Professor of Health Policy and Management, New York University, Wagner Graduate School of Public Service

Michael Schrunk, District Attorney, Multnomah County, Oregon

Michael Smith, Professor, University of Wisconsin Law School

Context

Eric Lane: Let's start at the beginning. What are the conditions that have created problem-solving courts? Why do they exist?

Hon. Judith Kaye: Unquestionably the first modern day reality that you have to look at is the numbers of cases in the state courts, which are huge. Then there is the nature of the cases—there are not only more of them, but they've changed. We've witnessed the breakdown of the family and of other traditional safety nets. So what we're seeing in the courts is many, many more substance abuse cases. We have a huge number of domestic violence cases. We have many, many more quality-of-life crimes. And it's not just the subject of the cases that's different. We get a lot of repeat business. We're recycling the same people through the system. And things get worse. We know from experience that a drug possession or an assault today could be something considerably worse tomorrow.

Hon. Kathleen Blatz: If we're going to look at the conditions that have brought problem-solving courts into being, I think I would start with the public. Clearly there has been an increasing fear of crime. Census data show that your chance of being a victim of crime is actually the same today as it was in 1973. This means that in 25 years we have not affected your chance of being a victim. We've greatly increased your chance of being arrested and prosecuted. We've filled our prisons. But your chance of being a victim has not changed. The public is shocked when they hear that. It really begs a lot of questions about what we're doing in the criminal justice system and whether it is working. And judges are very frustrated. They see these problems. I think the innovation that we're seeing now is a result of judges processing cases like a vegetable factory. Instead of cans of peas, you've got cases. You just move 'em, move 'em, move 'em. One of my colleagues on the bench said: "You know, I feel like I work for McJustice: we sure aren't good for you, but we are fast."

Hon. Legrome Davis: I run the felony criminal courts in Philadelphia. In the course of one year, I had 5,000 felony defendants plead in front of me and get sentenced. I spent the next five years of my life watching them come back to court with an array of problems. The challenge in my mind is how to address that situation. Really what we're talking about are the things that probation was designed to do. But in a jurisdiction like Philadelphia, with a probation department that has 45,000 people under supervision, it's just not possible for them to bring services to bear in a concentrated, meaningful way.

Hon. James Cayce: The reason that the mental health court in Seattle got started is, unfortunately, the reason that a lot of court innovations have taken place. And that's because of a tragic incident. In our case, there was a high-profile murder committed by a mentally-ill person who had previously been to court on a misdemeanor case. This tragedy was the immediate reason people in Seattle were interested in the mental health court, but there were other reasons as well. It was clear that the system had totally failed the mentally-ill population.

Hon. Truman Morrison: It is terribly odd that America is looking to the judicial branch to solve these problems. It seems to me that in very large measure, this is happening because of the abject failure of the other branches of government.

John Goldkamp: As a student of change in the courts, I think there are some practical forces that have impelled change as well. One is the drug epidemic and the war against drugs in the 1980s, which had the effect of blowing up many criminal justice systems. The second is the widespread overcrowding in the nation's correctional facilities, which has also put a strain on the system and raised serious questions about what we're going to do about delivering justice. We can thank these two factors for forcing innovation in all sorts of areas.

Michael Schrunk: When I was first elected DA, I thought I knew best. I went out to the neighborhoods and I just knew that murders, rapes, and armed robberies were the most important thing to residents. They handed me my lunch. They talked about quality-of-life crimes. I think that's what led me to push strongly for drug courts, for mental health courts, and for community courts—a desire to get out there and re-establish the rule of law in the community. You know, it's all well and good for us to read about the Microsoft trial or the O.J. Simpson trial or some other sensational trial, but that's a very, very small percentage of what goes on in the world of our constituents. I strongly believe we've got to work on public credibility, because a lot of citizens, quite frankly, don't think judges are relevant.

New Roles

Lane: What's so new about what judges are doing in problem-solving courts?

Hon. Cindy Lederman: It seems to me that the public is now coming to the courts and asking for solutions to problems like crime, domestic violence, and substance abuse. If we as judges accept this challenge, we're no longer the referee or the spectator. We're a participant in the process. We're not just looking at the offense any more. We're looking more and more at the best interests, not just of the defendant, but of the defendant's family and the community as well. This is quite a leap. It's not traditional. And not every judge can or should do this. It can be a disaster to have the wrong judge sitting in a problem-solving court. It's much more difficult than sitting in a normal courtroom. You need to read more than the law. You need a lot more courage as well, because you will be subject to tremendous criticism from your colleagues. "Are you being impartial? Do you know too much so that you can no longer be impartial?" I can't tell you how many times I've heard that. Which leads me to one of my favorite quotes, which is, "The judiciary is the only profession that exalts ignorance."

Kaye: I've never understood that. I've been an appellate judge for more than 16 years. I've decided a lot of Uniform Commercial Code cases. I love the Uniform Commercial Code. I read a lot about it. Am I doing something unethical? Is the domestic violence judge who tries to make himself an informed person on the very difficult issue of domestic violence doing something unethical?

Morrison: I'm puzzled by some of the things that Judge Lederman said. I don't understand why it is that only a few of her colleagues would be fit to be in one of these special courts. I hope that it isn't because only a few of them share her ideological view of how you approach domestic violence or how you approach drug abuse, because if that's true, I think that's very, very worrisome.

Schrunk: I agree wholeheartedly that not every judge can be a problem-solving court judge. My public defender and I have to go out and recruit judges, literally, with the blessing of our presiding judge, to see if they'd be willing to do a drug court, to do a community court. We get turned down by some of my former deputies, some of my public defender's former deputies. What we're looking for is a proactive judge as opposed to a reactive judge, someone who can preserve the core values of the judiciary, but still be a risk-taker. I think there needs to be a recognition that this is non-traditional judging, just as I tell my young lawyers fresh out of law school who want to slug felons that this is non-traditional prosecuting. And I suspect deputy public defenders find out when they serve a tour in problem-solving courts that it's non-traditional defending, too. We're not preparing people in law schools for this.

Kaye: The suggestion is on the table that there is some sort of ideology that makes a good problem-solving judge. I thought it would be worthwhile hearing from one of the problem-solving judges.

Lederman: I think there's an ideology. There's a personality as well. There are many judges who are reluctant to speak human to human to the people that appear before them. Those judges are inappropriate for a problem-solving court. A judge has to feel that it's the responsibility of the judiciary to engage in this sort of work and have the personality to engage human beings from the bench. Not every judge has these characteristics.

Morrison: I still don't have a picture yet of who the ideal person for this job is. It strikes me that it ought to be a good judge—someone who is open to other people's ideas, who listens, who is informed, who is impartial. All of us have colleagues who are brilliant and colleagues who are boors. Obviously, we don't want bad judges in these courts. If we put aside the real bad people who probably shouldn't be on the bench anyway, most judges could do this job, many more than do. By way of example, let me tell you about a colleague of mine on the bench. He's actually the senior judge in our court, who everybody would define as a traditional judge, to the extent we all have a stereotype of that. Years ago, he served as the judge in our local drug court. Yesterday, he absolutely shocked me by saying that his year on the drug court was the single most meaningful experience he's had in 22 years of being a judge. I said: "Gosh, that surprises me. Why is that?" He said: "Because in many ways I was able, with complete fidelity to all my principles, to do a better job of being a judge in that context than I ever was doing anything else." I say this just to underline that if we're doing this right, it shouldn't be a tiny little fraternity and sorority of select jurists who are up to the task.

Hon. Judy Harris Kluger: I don't think you need a particular ideology. That would be terrible. I do believe that, except for our problem judges, most judges could do this job well. In my experience, once the Midtown Community Court got started in New York, judges said: "Could I sit there?" These judges were very different, but the common denominator was they were tired of having their competence evaluated on how many arraignments they could do. You know, for a long time my claim to fame was that I arraigned 200 cases in one session. That's ridiculous. When I was arraigning cases, I'd be handed the papers, say the sentence is going to be five days, ten days, whatever, never even looking at the defendant. At a community court, I'm able to look up from the papers and see the person standing in front of me. It takes two or three more minutes, but I think a judge is much more effective that way.

Structure

Morrison: I'm concerned about the power that judges have and I'm concerned about giving judges the ability to make decisions that are just borne of their individual world view. I don't think we should free judges to leave their traditional role and be informed only by their own personal definition of what justice is. I spent my life as a lawyer walking into courtrooms with the law on my side and I would lose, and the reason I would lose was the jurist I appeared in front of thought he knew justice when he saw it. That kind of anarchy is what I don't want in courts. I don't think that has to in any way inhibit the creative role of problem-solving courts, but I think it's a risk that we need to pay attention to. We need to pay attention to the integrity of the court's adjudicatory function. It may in fact be true that 99 percent of the cases that we're talking about here today are resolved through plea bargains. But it is essential to the integrity of the courts that we maintain the ability to serve the other one percent, however silly that may seem. We should never lose sight of the need to be faithful to the courts' ability to service the minorities. We run this institution in part to maintain the integrity of a process that isn't used very often to determine disputes in ways other than plea bargains.

Blatz: But you could set up a system to deal with the 99 percent of the cases much more effectively, which we have not done.

Morrison: I agree. Part of what I'm talking about is a function of architecture. I talked before about how I think it's surprising that we turn to courts to solve problems. When you try and channel the energies of social change into the judicial branch, it's not a good fit. Judges' own personal world views shouldn't be unleashed under the guise of special courts.

Lederman: I still think we need to be vigilant about who we put in these courts. After 10 years of sitting on the bench, it seems to me that every day I have a tremendous ability to harm people. I think the ability to harm could be enhanced by the very nature of a problem-solving court.

Lane: Could you expand a little bit on the potential for causing damage?

Lederman: Well, one thing, I'm not sitting back and watching the parties and ruling. I'm making comments. I'm encouraging. I'm making judgment calls. I'm getting very involved with families. I'm making clinical decisions to some extent, with the advice of experts. So I have much greater opportunities, I think, to harm someone than I would if I just sat there, listened, and said guilty or not guilty.

Kaye: As an administrator, I don't want the arrogant, anarchist judge in any court. I can tell you, though, how energizing a problem-solving court can be for judges. They are excited about this not because they are re-engineering the world, but because they feel they are exercising a meaningful role as a judge.

Blatz: It seems to me that a bad judge can do less damage in a problem-solving court than they can do unfettered in the normal system. Once a problem-solving court is up and running, ownership and responsibility are shared. In a drug court, it isn't the judge by himself who's coming up with the rules about graduated sanctions or how to respond to violations—it's done in consultation with the defense and prosecution. Nobody wants a bad judge. But I think a mediocre judge can look a heck of a lot better in a problem-solving court where systems are in place than they can in a traditional court, where they can do absolutely anything.

Tradition

Richard Cappalli: I'd like to bring some conventional thinking into this discussion. What I'd like to do is bring in the thinking of Chief Justice John

Marshall as he described the judicial role in 1824.

Kaye: I'd like to take him to the criminal court of the City of New York.

Cappalli: I understand that. But there is some wisdom in old ways of thinking. So what I'd like to do is to bring a quotation into this discussion from *Osborne v. The Bank of the United States*. It goes like this: "Judicial power as contradistinguished from the powers of the laws has no existence. Courts are the mere instruments of the law and can will nothing. When they are said to exercise a discretion, it is a mere legal discretion, a discretion to be exercised in discerning the course prescribed by law. When that is discerned, it is the duty of the court to follow it. Judicial power is never exercised for the purpose of giving effect to the will of the judge, always for the purpose of giving effect to the will of the law." I think we have to talk about the ancient values of our legal system and how one goes about protecting not only defendants, but protecting judges from lawsuits and recusal motions. When judges move out of the box of the law and into working with individual defendants, transforming them from law-breaking citizens into law-abiding citizens, we have to worry. Because what has always protected the bench has been the law. Whenever a judge is approached by a disgruntled individual saying, "How could you do that?" The judge always says: "That wasn't me speaking—that was the law." If we take the mantle of the law's protections off of the judges and put them into these new roles, we have to worry about judicial neutrality, independence, and impartiality.

Kluger: I don't believe for one minute that these courts are operating outside the law. The statutes allow us to do what we're doing—to refer and monitor people in treatment, to utilize community service as a sanction. It may be a different world than Judge Marshall's world, but it's not outside of the law.

Kaye: I find myself a little hung up on nomenclature here. What is a traditional judge today, anyway? The other day I was meeting with John Feinblatt of the Center for Court Innovation and he drew three boxes on a sheet of paper. The number one box is John Marshall and the traditional view of the role of courts. The number two box is what's going on in reality today—the plea bargains, the mill court, McJustice. We're not functioning in the number one box any more in the state courts, except in 1 percent of the cases. For the most part, in the overwhelming numbers, the traditional judge today is in box number two, pleading cases at arraignment. Then we have box number three, which is the problem-solving box. Now, if you compare the number one box to the number three box you might well have the concerns of Justice Marshall. But try comparing the number two box to the number three box. It's quite a different picture, isn't it, professor?

Cappalli: I think John Marshall would say that hopefully in that second box, even though mass justice is being applied, all judges are committed to applying the law, and that every decision that the judge makes is guided by New York State statutes that are sufficiently clear to tell him what to do and sentencing guidelines that are sufficiently clear to tell him how to act.

Ellen Schall: I would say that this notion of the traditional model as an ideal is actually dangerous, because it misses the point that it wasn't working. The reason we got into problem-solving courts is because it wasn't working for a judge to sit there and process, to do McJustice. That's not a thing you would ask a trained person to participate in. It's not a good use of anyone's time. I think we have to begin from the notion that the system from which the problem-solving courts have emerged was a failure on any count. It wasn't a legal success. It wasn't a social success. It wasn't working.

The Role of Attorneys

Lane: Professor Cappalli has summoned the ghost of John Marshall so it seems only appropriate to turn to Professor Nelson. As a legal historian, do you have any comments to add?

William Nelson: There have always been institutions possessed of the coercive power of government that have performed the kinds of functions we see today in problem-solving courts. For example, the justices of the peace throughout the 18th, 19th, and early 20th century were remarkably like the judges we're hearing about today, with one difference. The structures that were there to help these justices engage in improving behavior were family structures, community structures, and not professional psychiatrists, social workers, and the like. But that seems to me to be not a comment on the judiciary, but a comment on the changing structure of American society. There's one other major difference. In the 1940s, 50s, and 60s, we introduced lawyers into the petty courts, which seems to me to profoundly change what they do. I think there were reasons why as a society we did this. There were reasons why we cared about due process. There were reasons why we thought it was important to introduce John Marshall's idea of the rule of law to the more marginal people of society. There were obviously some enormously high costs to be paid for introducing lawyers into this process, because what the introduction of lawyers into this process did was to destroy what had been an ongoing system in which courts were problem solvers. So it's a trade-off, and I think we need to keep these trade-offs in mind as we decide whether we're doing the right thing with these problem-solving courts.

Michael Smith: One of the things that judges and courts are particularly good at, when they're not just milling people, is fact finding. But a fact-finding court is heavily reliant on advocates if it's any good. The presentation of evidence—and the judge's ability to make findings of fact about the plausibility of various potential interventions—is something that seems to be missing with problem-solving courts. I think one of the advantages courts have is the opportunity to test assertions. If we don't figure out a way to take advantage of that, then we're not going to have very good problem-solving courts. The courts will be no better than the social service clinics, which have failed to address these problems. So the adversary system and the presence of defense counsel are of enormous value in problem solving.

Lane: Are we witnessing some failures of zealous advocacy in these courts? There's lots of talk that the team approach at drug courts undermines counsel's ability to effectively advocate for their clients. Is getting along a threat to the core values of courts or attorneys?

Schrunk: Well, concerns about zealous prosecution can be defeated by results. Good, hard-core evaluation can help explain why dismissing 1,500 drug cases during the course of a year at the drug court is a better end product than 1,500 convictions in a regular court. As for zealous defense, I've not seen defense counsel roll over. I learned long ago that I've got to have defense counsel at the table to keep me from overreaching.

Blatz: I think what you need at problem-solving courts are attorneys, on both sides, who are willing to say, "Judge, our normal procedure is not going to work in this case," and then have the judge make an independent decision.

Schrunk: Exactly. That's why you need defense counsel and you need the prosecutor there. But it's only going to be a small percentage of cases where attorneys need to stand up and holler.

Blatz: I think the only difference in terms of the zealousness of advocacy in a problem-solving court is that you might get obsequiousness out of familiarity with the judge and the team approach. I know attorneys can sometimes get too close to the judge or to the court and then they feel like they can't make challenges. That's a risk. But in a non-problem-solving court you can get obsequiousness out of fear. When I was a trial judge, I saw attorneys intimidated before I had even opened my mouth. It's the same problem.

Ex Parte Communication

Cait Clarke: I want to talk about an experience I had with my criminal justice class recently when we went to visit a drug court. We were brought behind the scenes when all of the players were at the table and the negotiating was going on about case resolutions. My students turned to me and asked: where's the defense lawyer? They weren't in the room.

Kluger: It shouldn't happen. It was a mistake, I would imagine, and there should never be a discussion about a case and a defendant without the prosecutor and the defense counsel being present.

Lane: So Judge Kluger's point is that this is bad practice but not necessarily a byproduct of the problem-solving court, that ex parte communication is a risk in every courtroom.

Blatz: I think the chances of ex parte communication increase greatly in a problem-solving court, but to the degree that people engage in these practices, I think it's totally inappropriate under any model.

Clarke: I just want to clarify, because I don't think the drug court judge thought he was having an ex parte experience, and I'll tell you why. The judge felt that because the defendant had already pled guilty that the court was no longer in the adjudicatory mode. He felt that they were in the therapeutic stage. I think he thought that they were simply caring for a client.

Kluger: I do agree there is an ex parte risk with problem-solving courts, but I don't think it's the traditional risk of the judge and prosecutor talking without the defense attorney. The risk is that the judge will talk with clinical staff without either of the parties present.

Morrison: What concerns me is that a problem-solving court would decide that the most effective way to deliver treatment is by having the professionals decide it without littering up the room with obstructionist lawyers.

Smith: My view is that if judges who are sitting in these roles don't make sure that they've got defense counsel and prosecutors who are prepared to say, "Judge, that's bull," when some treatment professional comes in and says this is the right thing to do, then the judge is really without the special advantages that courts offer when trying to make solutions to problems in individual cases. If you don't have that, then why the hell do we have the court?

Candace McCoy: I think we probably have a consensus here about the inappropriateness of ex parte communication. My concern with these courts is broader. The issue that concerns me is the coerciveness of the trial penalty itself. Now, we can't solve that one today, I think that's pretty clear. But I think we could start with the physician's ethical admonition, "First, do no harm." It's pretty bad right now in terms of the coerciveness of the guilty plea system, so you don't want to make it worse under a problem-solving court system.

Kathleen Clark: Lawyers don't have that obligation, at least not explicitly. And in fact, many lawyers see as an integral part of their job the obligation to do harm to others in order to help their client. So while I'm not sure whether the "do no harm" notion applies to courts, it clearly doesn't apply to lawyers. But I want to come back to this ex parte question, because I think there is another issue worth exploring, and it relates to what Judge Morrison was saying earlier about ideology. Problem-solving judges are expected, I think, to become knowledgeable about a social problem and about the received wisdom concerning the most appropriate ways to address that problem. In the process, they are engaging in conversations, not necessarily about a particular case, but about classes of cases. Now, that's not prohibited by the Code, but judges are rightly sensitive about it. And the more the caseload is specialized, the more there's a tension between this received wisdom—which some people might identify as ideology—and the notion of impartiality that's expressed through ex parte prohibitions.

Blatz: This notion that Professor Clark brings up, that knowledge is bias, I have a hard time with. Ignorant people can be biased and they can have an agenda, as can knowledgeable people. So I have never understood why we need to make sure judges are ignorant. That is the old model and I just don't buy it.

Going to Scale

Lane: Let's look at the institutional issues raised by these courts. How do we begin to integrate problem-solving courts into the fabric of a state court system?

Schall: I guess I would say three things. The first is that before you go to scale, you want to be thoughtful about what you take to scale. You don't want to just take everything that exists and multiply it. The second point is to ask what is the role of problem-solving courts in system change outside of the courtroom, in the mental health system and the domestic violence system? I don't see much point in fixing the family court in any given jurisdiction if you don't also increase the capacity of the child welfare system to be effective. The third point for me is what are the implications for the rest of the judicial system? If drug courts are very busy trying to connect individuals with their families, then why in the rest of the criminal court do we incarcerate women for 10 days for some petty offense and have them lose their children to the foster care system and then have to work for years to get them back? Why, if we've learned something in some part of the court, why can't we move it into the rest of the court?

Smith: It seems to me that there are two different ways to go to scale. One is to use problem-solving courts as laboratories, importing what we've learned about practice to the rest of the court system to improve the way it does business. The other is to build a new system devoted to proliferating problem-solving courts. That choice may turn out to be a critical one.

Schall: I want to push back on going to scale. I think Michael asked an important question. He suggested one way of going to scale is to take what we know and influence the rest of the courts, which may mean that problem-solving courts would continue to exist or they may not. Or going to scale could mean every court system in this country should have some percentage of its business conducted in problem-oriented courts. I don't think it's clear what we mean by "going to scale."

Schrunk: I look at going to scale this way—I think a lot of jurisdictions are going to reach critical mass on problems, whether it's drugs, whether it's mental health, whether it's quality-of-life crime, and they're going to take a step back and say, "Can't we do things better?" There's a big risk, particularly for the judiciary, in taking this step, and I think the risk is failure. I think the challenge is taking the step and still holding onto our core values. I think one of the vital components in doing so are the prosecution and defense, because I think those two advocates are not going to let a judge run roughshod and sell a program that just doesn't work.

Cappalli: Cut me off if I slow down the march toward scale. I came into this relatively ignorant of problem-solving courts, and I thought that might be a good idea, to bring in somebody who can take some fresh looks at these things. I see a number of very serious problems. One of them is coercion. It strikes me that you've got a terrible problem of coercion and consent in problem-solving courts. The second thing I worry about is the absence of structure. It seems to me that the "good judge" might be the judge who feels comfortable bending the rules to get to what that judge feels is the correct result. Well, as a professor of civil procedure, it worries me because we've spent hundreds of years devising procedures to ensure that things are done fairly. One final problem is paternalism. It strikes me that these courts are highly paternalistic. What they're going to do is to reform individuals, with some suspect consent on their part, by putting their superior expertise to work deciding who this individual is, what this individual's problems are, and what set of services can best help this individual re-integrate himself or herself into the community. That is an extraordinarily paternalistic system. Now, that isn't necessarily bad. But it is something that deserves discussion.

Kaye: I'm not sure what choice we have. You read the papers, you know what's coming into our courts. The political branches are choosing to put more and more cases into the courts. The state courts are the gatehouses of the law. The federal courts are the manor houses of the law. We are dealing with the population that we have and we are simply trying to do the best job that we can. The truth is, we're trying to improve the system, and maybe disaggregating a little bit is a good way to do it. The system is so massive, we can't declare it a failure and walk away from it. Nobody's doing that.

Goldkamp: This reminds me of a discussion that I participated in in the early 90s. I was invited to a meeting of judges and I watched them hold a debate about drug courts. Some said: "I don't know if we should be doing this kind of thing; it's just not what judges are supposed to do." And others said: "Excuse me, where do you live?" It was very, very informative. That was a good while ago. So I find today's discussion anachronistic. I think what we have now is not a bunch of little hobbies that judges have in isolated jurisdictions, but rather a paradigm shift that larger court systems are trying to come to grips with. They're at your door step. The question isn't: Gosh, are courts supposed to be doing this? It's: What are you going to do about it? How does it fit in? It's no longer a question of whether this should have been invented. They're here.

Creating Good Courts:
Effectiveness, Fairness and
Problem-Solving Justice

Shortly after I was named director of the Center for Court Innovation in 2002, I was invited to speak at a symposium on problem-solving courts at Columbia Law School. I knew going in that many of the other speakers would be hostile towards these new experiments. One of the sharpest critics was James Nolan, a professor at Williams College who had written an essay attacking drug courts in particular. I was given the job of responding to Nolan. This short essay is what I produced. It represents my most concise response to one of the central criticisms that problem-solving courts have engendered: that in a misguided effort to do good, they trammel the rights of defendants. This essay originally appeared in American Criminal Law Review, Summer 2004, Volume 41, Issue No. 3. It is reproduced here with minimal changes.

The central argument of James Nolan's essay, "Redefining Criminal Courts: Problem-Solving and the Meaning of Justice," seems to be that problem-solving courts have become so blinded by the seductive rhetoric of "therapeutic jurisprudence" that they have lost sight of fundamental legal traditions like due process and proportionality.[86] At the heart of Nolan's critique is the concern that, if the advocates of problem-solving courts have their way, treatment will somehow come to replace fairness as a central value of the American justice system. It is not just the unintended consequences of judicially-mandated treatment that Nolan is concerned about. He writes: "Drug courts are regularly defended on the grounds of program efficacy ... to enter into a debate about whether drug courts are or are not efficacious is

---

[86] Nolan seems fuzzy about the differences between drug courts and other kinds of problem-solving courts, such as community courts, domestic violence courts, mental health courts and others. Despite the title of his article, he primarily focuses on drug courts to the exclusion of these other types of initiatives. See James L. Nolan, "Redefining Criminal Courts: Problem-Solving and the Meaning of Justice," 40 *American Criminal Law Review* (2003), pp. 1541-1565.

to miss the larger point. The more important question is what effect does a preoccupation with efficacy have on the meaning of justice?"

Nolan seems to be suggesting that any effort by courts to focus on the efficacy of sentencing is inappropriate. It is hard to imagine that we would create a criminal justice system that never asked whether the sanctions it metes out have the desired impact on offenders (or on the public), but if you follow Nolan's logic, that seems to be where you end up.

To illustrate his point that problem-solving courts are attempting a "radical judicial reorientation," Nolan cites a number of harrowing stories from the frontlines of American drug courts—stories of judges coercing defendants into treatment, of courts that use Orwellian double speak when sanctioning offenders, of drug court advocates seeking to extend the authority of the court into the homes of drug court participants.[87] The cumulative impact of these anecdotes is to paint a dire portrait of drug courts. Indeed, reading Nolan, one might easily conclude that drug courts are, to quote from another critic, "a caricature of a courtroom, in which judges are anything but impartial, defense lawyers are virtually invisible, prosecutors are making most of the decisions about who may or may not participate ... and service providers are the primary information source."[88]

As Nolan's stories of bullying judges and the importation of 12-step vocabulary into the courtroom make clear, it is possible to find some examples of shoddy practice happening in drug courts across the country. It would be foolish not to admit this. It would be even more foolish to try to defend such practices. The truth is that any system staffed by idiosyncratic and fallible humans will occasionally result in bad practice. Bad practice should be rooted out of problem-solving courts, just the way it should be rooted out of conventional courts.

Nolan does a great service to the field by identifying some of the more egregious examples of misbehavior in drug courts. He fails to make the case, however, that bad practice is somehow intrinsic to drug courts. Put simply, there is no evidence to suggest that shoddy judging and substandard lawyering are any more widespread in drug courts than in conventional state courts. Quite the contrary. There is good reason to believe that these closely-watched experiments, with their emphasis on state-of-the-art technology, accountability and formalized systems of sanctions and rewards, actually reduce the potential for judges and other court players to run amok. Beyond the issue of bad practice, Nolan's critique of drug courts raises a number of questions.

---

[87] Nolan. "Redefining Criminal Courts," p. 1560.

[88] Anthony Thompson. "Courting Disorder: Some Thoughts on Community Courts," 10 *Washington University Journal of Law and Policy* (2002), pp. 97-98.

Are problem-solving courts examples
of therapeutic jurisprudence?

Nolan's argument is built on the assumption that drug courts are "a direct application of therapeutic jurisprudence theory." As articulated by its two leading proponents, David Wexler and Bruce Winick, therapeutic jurisprudence has been defined as "the use of social science to study the extent to which a legal rule or practice promotes the psychological and physical well-being of the people it affects."[89]

To support his claim that drug courts are real-life examples of therapeutic jurisprudence in action, Nolan relies on a law review article by two drug court judges (and a co-author) that argues that "without being conscious of its use" drug courts have been applying therapeutic jurisprudence to the problems of addicted criminal defendants. Thus, therapeutic jurisprudence provides "the legal and jurisprudential foundations of this new criminal justice concept."[90]

There are good reasons why some drug court practitioners have been attracted to therapeutic jurisprudence: it is outcome-oriented, multi-disciplinary, emphasizes empirically verifiable results, and asks practitioners to think outside the confines of individual cases. That is all part and parcel of the daily work of not only drug courts, but community courts, mental health courts and other problem-solving initiatives as well.

While there is significant overlap between therapeutic jurisprudence and problem-solving courts, it would be a mistake to conflate the two. Although some drug court practitioners have embraced therapeutic jurisprudence, many others blanch at the concept. Their concerns are two-fold. First, they worry that therapeutic jurisprudence is a political liability as a label, an instant turn-off for those who, like Nolan, immediately conjure images of *A Clockwork Orange* and judges leading 12-step programs.

More substantively, there is a concern that the "therapeutic justice" label does not adequately describe either the origins or the methods of problem-solving courts—that it places these courts too squarely in the business of rehabilitation. Problem-solving courts are, of course, concerned with rehabilitation and they do, in fact, rely on therapeutic interventions to change the behavior of offenders. But this represents just part of their work. Much of what problem-solving courts do has no explicit therapeutic dimension. When community courts sentence low-level offenders to perform commu-

---

89   Christopher Slobogin. "Therapeutic Jurisprudence: Five Dilemmas to Ponder," in David B. Wexler and Bruce J. Winick, eds., *Law in a Therapeutic Key: Developments in Therapeutic Jurisprudence*, Carolina Academic Press, 1996, p. 769.

90   Peggy Fulton Hora, William G. Schma and John T.A. Rosenthal. "Therapeutic Jurisprudence and the Drug Treatment Court Movement: Revolutionizing the Criminal Justice System's Response to Drug Abuse and Crime in America," 74 *Notre Dame Law Review* 2 (January 1999), pp. 439-537.

nity service, it's not because they're trying to "heal" the offenders, it's because they want to pay back the local neighborhood that's been harmed by crime. When domestic violence courts require batterers to return to court for judicial monitoring of their compliance with orders of protection, it's not with any therapeutic intent, it's to try to make sure they don't continue to abuse their partners.

The point here is not to deny that there is a relationship between problem-solving courts and therapeutic justice, but rather to suggest that it is a more complicated one than Nolan's reading suggests. Nolan's article simply elides the differences. It also elides the differences between and among various problem-solving models. Drug courts are different than community courts. Community courts are different than mental health courts. Mental health courts are different than domestic violence courts. It is worth keeping these distinctions in mind before drawing broad conclusions.

Where are the defense attorneys?

Given Nolan's concerns about "possible violations of individual constitutional rights" in drug courts, it is worth spending a few moments looking at the role of defenders. Defense attorneys are explicitly charged with representing the interests of defendants in order to ensure the fairness of the justice system. What role do they play in these new experiments? Reading Nolan, it would be easy to come away with the impression that there were no defense attorneys in drug courts or that the ones who practice there are effectively bound and gagged by overzealous judges and prosecutors. This is simply not true.

The reality is that both drug courts and conventional state courts are fundamentally collaborative enterprises that require the active participation of prosecutors, judges and defenders if they are going to work. Simply put, defense attorneys could effectively shut down drug courts if they wanted to by refusing to participate or let their clients plead guilty and enter treatment. By and large, this hasn't happened of course. Why not? One answer can be found in a letter written by Daniel Greenberg, the head of the Legal Aid Society in New York City, to the *New York Law Journal*. In the letter, Greenberg argues on behalf of judge-driven alternative to incarceration programs like drug courts as compared to diversion programs that operate out of prosecutor's offices:

> Common sense tells us we are all better served when accused criminal defendants with addiction problems are treated rather than incarcerated for unconscionably long periods.... The Legal Aid Society has supported effective alternative to incarceration programs and we hope that their success will expand the willingness of others use them....We believe that

greater promise of fairness and success lies with returning discretion to judges to fashion appropriate remedies and programs.[91]

It would be facile to suggest that Greenberg's letter is emblematic of widespread enthusiasm for drug courts within the defender community; defenders have had a wide range of responses to drug courts—from open hostility to grudging acceptance to growing endorsement. But it is worth asking why defender agencies like the Legal Aid Society have expressed support, however conditional, for these programs.

By and large, good drug courts have included defenders in the planning process, giving them a seat at the table when determining eligibility criteria, treatment mandates and sanctioning schemes. Good drug courts have delivered what defenders have wanted from courts for years: treatment instead of incarceration for their clients. And good drug courts have not, in fact, lost sight of proportionality. The moment that drug courts start trying to send first-time offenders arrested for shoplifting to 18 months of in-patient treatment is the moment when public defenders will opt for trial instead of encouraging their clients to plea. Defenders vote with their feet—if drug courts didn't offer them (and their clients) a good deal, they wouldn't agree to play.

Compared to what?

What is the alternative to drug court? By implication, Nolan's article suggests that the alternative is a 'classical' due process model in which each case receives a full-blown adversarial trial.

The reality is that by and large our state courts no longer operate on a classical adversarial model (if indeed, they ever did). Writing in the late 1970s, author Malcolm Feeley described American courts this way: "Rather than hard-fought trials ending with harsh sentences for the guilty and vindication of the innocent, there are hardly any trials at all. Instead, there is a variety of informal dispositional practices, lenient sentences, and a general spirit of cooperation among supposedly adversarial agents."[92]

The process that Feeley is describing has led many—both within the criminal justice system and outside—to conclude that the courts engage in "revolving door justice." More than nine out of ten cases in state courts are resolved not by trial but by plea bargain.[93] Prosecutors and defenders have effectively been transformed into negotiators and deal-makers rather than

---

[91] Daniel L. Greenberg. "Prosecutors Are The Wrong Gatekeepers," *New York Law Journal*, letter to the editor, March 17, 2003.

[92] Malcolm M. Feeley. *The Process Is The Punishment: Handling Cases In A Lower Criminal Court*, Russell Sage Foundation, 1979, p. 244.

[93] Lindsey Devers. "Plea and Charge Bargaining: Research Findings," *Bureau of Justice Assistance* (2011), p. 1.

adversarial litigators. The most common form of punishment in state courts is, in fact, probation—close to half of felony offenders receive probation sentences. According to the U.S. Bureau of Justice Statistics, close to 15 percent of felony offenders also receive either drug treatment or community service mandates.[94] The bottom line is that, with or without problem-solving courts, the American criminal justice system is in the business of linking offenders to community-based services and supervision.

Courts may already be in the business of community-based sanctions, but they don't do a particularly good job of it. Probation caseloads in some cities are as high as 1,000 cases per officer.[95] It should come as little surprise that many probationers do not complete their sanctions, with a high number of rearrests.

As currently constructed, state courts are something less than a complete success in terms of either fairness or effectiveness. Business as usual in the courts can boast neither the due process protections of the classical adversarial model nor the emphasis on effective sentencing of the problem-solving model. Put simply, it is difficult to marshal a persuasive argument in favor of maintaining the status quo in the state courts.

Problem-solving courts represent an honest acknowledgment on the part of court administrators that the criminal justice system disposes of a high percentage of cases in a non-adversarial fashion and that the outcomes of these cases are often community-based treatment and supervision. Problem-solving courts didn't create these realities. What problem-solving courts have done is to improve court infrastructure, bringing new tools—technology, accountability mechanisms, research data, links to effective treatment regimens—into the courthouse. In doing so, problem-solving courts have improved the compliance of offenders with intermediate sanctions and encouraged courts to make greater use of alternatives to incarceration where appropriate. They have also changed the life-trajectories of thousands of offenders, helping them move from addiction to sobriety and from crime to law-abiding behavior.

All of which begs the question: Do problem-solving courts represent a "transformation of the adjudicative setting"? Do they alter the underlying theory of justice upon which our courts were founded? Or are they instead simply a change in methodology? Is it like doing addition with a calculator instead of by hand—the technology is different, but the underlying math is the same?

---

[94] Sean Rosenmerkel, Matthew Durose and Donald Farole. "Felony Defendants in State Courts, 2006," *Bureau of Justice Assistance* (December 2009), p. 8.

[95] Hugo Martin. "Probation Officers Strain to Keep Up With Caseloads," *Los Angeles Times*, July 26, 1999.

Is this a false choice?

Throughout his essay, Nolan sets up a dangerous dichotomy between efficacy and justice, between problem-solving and due process. Is this fair? Do we have to choose between them? Can the two co-exist comfortably side by side? What might this look like? A trip to the Red Hook Community Justice Center, a community court in Brooklyn that handles low-level criminal cases (along with selected civil and family court matters), offers some hints.

Visitors who sit in the courtroom at the Red Hook Community Justice Center are often surprised to discover that every defendant is represented by counsel and that the prosecution stands up on every case. On a typical day, the majority of the offenders who plead guilty to crimes like drug possession and shoplifting end up receiving alternative sanctions like community restitution, job training or treatment rather than incarceration. But a typical day at the Justice Center also finds a handful of cases dismissed because the prosecution has not presented a convincing case. And a typical day also sees a few cases receiving jail sentences because the judge deems the offenders a risk to public safety. What this suggests is that the problem-solving approach has not affected the court's ability to weigh the merits of each case. On the contrary, a problem-solving court like the one in Red Hook gives judges and attorneys more options so they can provide more individualized justice to defendants.

At the end of the day, if they are done right, problem-solving courts have the potential to improve not just the effectiveness of sentencing, but the fairness of case processing as well. The good problem solving courts are already achieving this vision. The challenge is to make sure that all problem-solving courts are good ones.

7 Moving Beyond Specialized Courtrooms

We know from experience that it can be enormously difficult to replicate problem-solving courts. So many things can go wrong. You can choose the wrong judge. You can run up against fundraising shortfalls. You can fail to win over local prosecutors. The list goes on and on. As challenging as replication can be, it is even more difficult to attempt to spread discrete ideas and practices that have been tested in problem-solving courts throughout a state court system. This essay, originally drafted in 2004, attempts to look at the challenges and opportunities afforded by statewide implementation.

Visitors to the Red Hook Community Justice Center in Brooklyn, New York are often overwhelmed by what they find there. That's not surprising— after all, the Justice Center is designed to be a state-of-the-art experiment in problem-solving justice.

Like the other first-generation problem-solving courts—which include drug courts, domestic violence courts, mental health courts, family treatment courts and others—the Red Hook Community Justice Center seeks to achieve several goals simultaneously. First and foremost, it is designed to make a difference in Red Hook, improving public safety and bolstering public confidence in justice. But the project has broader ambitions as well. The Justice Center is intended to be a conversation-starter, encouraging practitioners around the country to re-think business as usual in the courts and to test new approaches to cases where legal issues and social problems are inextricably intertwined.

Unfortunately, it is not uncommon for visitors' first reaction to Red Hook to be: "we can't do this in _____ (pick your city)." That's an understandable response to the new technology, architecture, on-site services and staffing resources at Red Hook, but it is not exactly the reaction that the project is intended to provoke.

It may be unrealistic—for reasons of philosophy or resources or political will—for most jurisdictions to replicate the Red Hook Community Justice Center model wholesale, but this does not mean that other places cannot adopt some of the problem-solving principles and practices that Red Hook has tested. All of which begs the question: What are the elements of a problem-solving court like Red Hook that are most easily replicable? And how might these components be implemented within conventional state courts rather than specialized, standalone courtrooms?

More and more, these are the kinds of questions that are occupying our thinking at the Center for Court Innovation. We are far from alone in grappling with these issues, however. Given the increasingly well-documented results of problem-solving courts, court systems across the country are also trying to come to grips with the problem-solving phenomenon and how it fits within the regular administration of justice.

One such court system is California's, which has made a significant investment in what is known locally as "collaborative justice."[96] Several years ago, the California Administrative Office of the Courts established a Collaborative Justice Courts Advisory Committee, which was charged with, among other things, looking at the application of problem-solving approaches on a statewide basis. Recognizing a shared interest in "going to scale," the California Administrative Office of the Courts and the Center for Court Innovation embarked upon a unique partnership designed to gather more information about how some of the practices associated with specialized, problem-solving courts might be applied within regular state courts.

Together, the Center for Court Innovation and the Administrative Office of the Courts of California convened a series of focus groups in both New York and California with judges who had presided over problem-solving courts. All told, 35 judges from drug courts, domestic violence courts, mental health courts and other specialized, problem-solving courtrooms participated in the study. While all of the judges had experience in problem-solving courts, all had since gone on to sit in "regular" criminal courts.[97]

Each of the focus groups featured broad-ranging conversation. At the most basic level, the underlying question driving the discussions was: Is it possible to uncouple problem-solving from specialization? That is, is it possible to practice problem-solving outside of the specialized courtroom setting? Encouragingly, the answer to this question appears to be "yes." Participants identified a number of practices that could be transferred from problem-solving courts to conventional courts. Problem-solving courts re-

---

[96] Robert V. Wolf. "California's Collaborative Courts: Building A Problem-Solving Judiciary," *Judicial Council of California* (2005).

[97] Donald Farole Jr., Nora Puffet, Michael Rempel and Francis Burne. "Can Innovation Be Institutionalized?" *Center for Court Innovation/California Administrative Office of the Courts* (2004).

quire a significant shift in judicial orientation, demanding that judges measure their success in new ways.

The operative question in most criminal courts is fairly straightforward: guilty or not guilty? By contrast, in a problem-solving court, judges are encouraged to ask an expanded array of questions: How can we improve public safety given the facts of this case? How do we address the harm to victims? What are the underlying problems of the defendant and how can we address them? The focus group participants suggested that this kind of problem-solving orientation could be adopted by judges in a variety of court settings.

Problem-solving courts have sought to expand the menu of sanctioning options available to judges by creating new links with community-based social service providers (e.g. drug treatment, job training, adult education). The focus groups suggested that improving access to, and coordination of, social services was crucial to doing problem-solving within conventional courts.[98]

Rather than relying on prosecutors and defenders for all of their information, problem-solving judges often directly engage with defendants as part of their effort to encourage behavior modification. The focus group judges regarded this as one of the easiest practices to transfer to other types of court calendars. Problem-solving courts also rely on ongoing judicial supervision to help ensure the compliance of offenders with community-based sanctions. While acknowledging the time limitations of practicing judges, focus group participants thought that judges in conventional state courts could be encouraged to promote greater accountability in alternative sanctions by requiring offenders to return to court to report on their progress.[99]

Problem-solving courts have asked whether it is possible to achieve better outcomes in selected cases by reducing the adversarial nature of the courtroom and encouraging prosecutors and defenders to craft mutually agreeable case resolutions. There was a fair amount of conversation about this subject in the focus groups, with the consensus being that Family Court offered a particularly ripe area to promote increased collaboration among courtroom advocates.

So what's the bad news? Participants in the focus group identified a number of significant obstacles to the spread of problem-solving justice. Generally, they can be grouped into two major categories. The first is resources. Effective problem-solving takes both time and money. Who is going to pay for the kinds of tools—technology, staffing, social service provision—that problem-solving requires?

---

[98] Farole, Jr. et al., "Can Innovation Be Institutionalized?" p. 9.

[99] Farole, Jr. et al., "Can Innovation Be Institutionalized?" p. 10.

The second major hurdle is philosophical. Problem-solving in the courts requires the active engagement of attorneys and judges, many of them deeply invested in the traditional approach to case processing. How do we convince them that problem-solving isn't antithetical to American legal values, that courts can perform their traditional roles—weighing the merits of each case, safeguarding the rights of individual citizens and ensuring that laws are obeyed—while also attempting to address the problems of individuals and communities?

As the focus groups make clear, courts are by design the most tradition-oriented of our government institutions. But this is by no means the end of the obstacles. Court systems are also sprawling bureaucracies that do not lend themselves to centralized control. A number of factors—including the fact that many judges are elected, the importance of preserving the independence of the judiciary, and the inter-dependent nature of the justice system—stand in the way of any reform idea, no matter how good, spreading quickly and broadly throughout a state court system.

Cultural change within the courts is going to take time—and it won't come easy. Replicating discrete problem-solving courts is one thing. Attempting to spread problem-solving values, principles, and approaches throughout a state court system is quite another.

Recognizing the challenges, there are six strategic investments that problem-solving advocates—both those within the courts (judges, attorneys, administrators) and those outside the courts (foundations, think tanks, academics)—might want to consider as they seek to influence the culture of state courts over the long haul.

1. Technology. At the core of the problem-solving approach is a reliance on data to identify problems, improve operations, promote accountability, and document results. Institutionalizing problem-solving will require a deep commitment to data collection, analysis, and dissemination. One of the best ways to promote problem-solving is to build effective management information systems and to create new performance measures for courts. This means providing administrators with regular research reports that detail not just how many cases are handled and how fast, but problem-solving indicators as well: How many individuals received treatment mandates? How many were linked to community service? What was their compliance? How many have been rearrested for new crimes? By asking these questions on a regular basis, administrators can begin to change the institutional culture of the court system.

2. Training. Institutionalizing problem-solving will require judges, clerks, attorneys, court officers and other court players to change their standard operating practice. You can't ask professionals, many of whom have been in their current jobs for decades, to do this without showing them how—and why. Training is crucial. States should develop standard curricula to introduce all judges to problem-solving. This could include the history of problem-solving and a detailed exploration of the methods employed by problem-solving judges. Curricula could also include a component on judicial ethics to help define the boundaries of appropriate judicial behavior in this new context. States should invest in training clerks and court administrators in problem-solving as well.

3. *Incentives.* State court administrators have a particularly important role to play if problem-solving is going to spread more broadly. First and foremost, they can use their bully pulpit to explain the value of the problem-solving approach and encourage its practice. Just as important, they can reward those who engage in problem-solving. A variety of incentives are possible, including salary increases, public recognition, choice assignments/promotion, travel opportunities, and prime office space. Using these kinds of levers aggressively will send a strong signal to those within a state court system that problem-solving work is valued.

4. *Ongoing R&D.* History tells us that today's innovation is tomorrow's conventional wisdom. To stay at the cutting edge, state court systems must continue to invest in seeking out new ideas, questioning accepted practices and testing new approaches even as they attempt to go to scale with problem-solving innovation. In this way, they can guard against the danger of institutionalization becoming bureaucratization. One of the lessons from statewide implementation efforts in other fields is the value of creating an intermediary authority charged with the responsibility of promoting the idea of change—providing technical assistance, disseminating best practices, and serving as an information clearinghouse.

5. *Law Schools.* Because today's students are tomorrow's judges and attorneys, law schools are a crucial vehicle for advancing the cause of problem-solving. Already, problem-solving has started to sneak into law schools on an ad-hoc basis thanks to judges and other adjunct faculty. The trick is to figure out how to build on this progress to make problem-solving part of the standard legal education across the country.

6. *Communications.* The court system doesn't operate in a vacuum. It is affected by a variety of external forces, including policymakers in the executive and legislative branches, the media and public opinion (not to mention the opinions of those who staff the courts). For all of these reasons, it is important to have a communications strategy in place to support the institutionalization of problem-solving. This means looking for every possible opportunity—PSAs, op-eds, public events—to spread the gospel of problem-solving justice.

Over time, these kinds of investments have the potential to achieve a significant shift in the orientation of state courts. It is important to make clear, however, that even if all of these dominoes fall into place, there are limits to how far the problem-solving approach can realistically extend. It is difficult to imagine that every judge in every courtroom across an entire state is going to engage in something like problem-solving justice for every case. It is also difficult to imagine that state courts will want to abandon the idea of specialization entirely—there is likely to be an ongoing need for special approaches to certain kinds of problem cases.

Perhaps the best analogy for how problem-solving might spread comes from the world of art history. As the late Bruce Winick pointed out, there are interesting parallels between problem-solving courts and the impressionist movement. The advent of impressionism—which was widely reviled by critics at the start—didn't result in every painter suddenly producing art that looked exactly like Monet's. Rather, over time, painters began to take certain elements from impressionism—the use of color, the choice of subject matter, a move away from strict realism—and apply them to their own work. As the focus groups highlight, there are a range of problem-solving elements that might be spread—and indeed, are already being spread— through the judiciary in a similar fashion.

Encouragingly, it is worth noting that the 35 judges who participated in the focus groups are hardly alone in their interest in problem-solving. A few years back, we commissioned a survey by the University of Maryland's Survey Research Center.[100] More than 500 criminal court judges, randomly selected, participated in a phone survey. While most were unfamiliar with the term "problem-solving court," they were broadly supportive of a range of problem-solving activities. For example: Participants supported treatment as an alternative to incarceration for addicted, nonviolent offenders (77 percent agreed that treatment was more effective than jail). Judges overwhelmingly agreed that the bench should be involved in reducing drug abuse among defendants (91 percent). Judges cited the need for more information about past violence when deciding bail and sentences in domestic violence cases (90 percent agreed). Sixty-three percent of the judges surveyed said they should be more involved with community groups in addressing neighborhood safety and quality-of-life concerns.

All of this runs counter to the popular assumption that judges, concerned with neutrality and independence, are unwilling to engage with communities or address the problems of individual defendants and victims.

Moreover, a 2001 survey by the National Center for State Courts found strong support—particularly among African-American and Hispanic respondents—for common problem-solving strategies, including the hiring of treatment staff and social workers; bringing offenders back to court to

---

[100] Aubrey Fox. "And the Survey Says...: State Court Judges and Problem-Solving Courts," *Center for Court Innovation* (2001).

report on their progress in treatment; coordinating the work of local treatment agencies to help offenders; and bringing in relevant outside experts to help courts make more informed decisions. The report concluded:

> A solid majority of the public backs new court and judicial roles associated with problem-solving.... Support for these new roles is strongest among African-Americans and Latinos. For example, more than 80 percent of those groups support courts hiring counselors and social workers.... The highly positive response of African-Americans to changes that would increase the involvement of the courts in people's lives is a marked contrast with the negative views African-Americans generally have of judges and the courts.[101]

Even taken together, the existing research into public and judicial attitudes toward problem-solving courts just begins to scratch the surface of what we might learn about this new approach. Going forward, it is worth testing some of the operating assumptions of problem-solving advocates with regard to procedural fairness—how do defendants perceive problem-solving courts? Are judges and attorneys who practice in problem-solving settings more satisfied with their jobs than those who do not? How does interacting with a problem-solving court affect citizens' perceptions of courts?[102]

While there is much work to be done, it is already possible to say with a fair degree of confidence that there is a growing number of people, both inside and outside the court system, who are interested in exploring new approaches to justice. If problem-solving courts don't have judges and citizens on the same page yet, they at least have them reading from the same book.

---

[101]   David B. Rottman and Randall M. Hansen. "How Recent Court Users View the State Courts: Perceptions of African-American, Latinos and Whites," *National Center for State Courts* (May 2001), p. 3.

[102]   In recent years, researchers have begun to document that problem-solving courts do in fact improve perceptions of procedural justice. See for example M. Somjen Frazer. "Red Hook: The Impact of the Community Court Model on Defendant Perceptions of Fairness," *Center for Court Innovation* (September 2006); Rashida Abuwala and Donald Farole Jr. "The Perceptions of Self-Represented Tenants in a Community-Based Housing Court," 44 *Court Review: The Journal of the American Judges Association* 1/2 (2007); Shelli Rossman, et al. "The Multi-Site Drug Court Evaluation," *Urban Institute* (November 2011).

PART III

THE CHALLENGES
OF IMPLEMENTATION

8 Challenging Conventional Wisdom: Lessons from Failed Criminal Justice Reforms

Over the last several years, the field of criminal justice has become increasingly sophisticated about using evidence to improve practice and spread strategies that have been proven effective by research. Driven by the United States Department of Justice and others, the movement to embrace "evidence-based programs" has helped make criminal justice agencies around the country smarter, more sophisticated and, hopefully, more effective.

As important as it is to spread proven programs, it is also important to encourage continued innovation. In an effort to do this, I have spent a great deal of time over the past few years trying to demystify and destigmatize failure. This has included co-writing a book with Aubrey Fox (Trial & Error in Criminal Justice Reform: Learning from Failure, Urban Institute Press). And it has included a variety of lectures, conference panels and roundtables, one of which is documented here. This piece originally appeared in the now defunct Journal of Court Innovation in 2008.

Criminal justice literature is full of "best practices"—depictions of how drug courts reduced recidivism or Compstat helped lower crime rates in New York City or DNA testing enabled a culprit to be nabbed. And rightly so: success in any endeavor is difficult to achieve and deserves to be celebrated. This is especially true in criminal justice, where for too long practitioners labored under the widespread assumption that "nothing works" and that it was impossible to reduce crime or change the behavior of offenders.

In general, it is human nature to shout about new ideas that have succeeded—while failure is discussed in hushed whispers, if at all. In truth, we know that it is impossible to have trial without error. Nobody is perfect. Nearly every criminal justice agency has attempted projects that have fizzled or failed to meet expectations. If we want to encourage criminal justice officials to test new ideas and challenge conventional wisdom, we need to create a climate where failure is openly discussed. We need to learn from our failures (and partial successes), examining whether an initiative works for some groups but not for others and figuring out what was wrong with the underlying assumptions that led us to try such an approach.

Unfortunately, what little public discussion there is of criminal justice failure tends to focus on corruption or gross incompetence or specific cases with tragic outcomes. While these kinds of errors should be publicized (and, needless to say, avoided), they typically offer few meaningful lessons for would-be innovators. Far more helpful would be a probing examination of the kinds of failures where decent, well-intentioned people attempted to achieve something noble and difficult but fell short of their objectives for whatever reason.

In January 2007, the Center for Court Innovation and the U.S. Department of Justice's Bureau of Justice Assistance set out to conduct just this kind of an examination. The two agencies jointly convened a day-long roundtable in New York that brought together judges, court administrators, probation officials, prosecutors, police chiefs, and defense attorneys from across the country to discuss lessons they have learned from projects that did not succeed. The goal of this effort was not to give out grades, point fingers or assess blame. Rather, the goal of the roundtable was to gather experienced and thoughtful criminal justice professionals to take a deeper look at failed reform efforts and attempt to extract concrete lessons that might aid the next generation of innovators, as well as those who authorize and fund innovation. In so doing, the Center for Court Innovation and the Bureau of Justice Assistance sought to send a message that failure, while not desirable, is sometimes inevitable and even acceptable, provided that it is properly analyzed and used as a learning experience.

The roundtable, which was moderated by Frank Hartmann from Harvard University's John F. Kennedy School of Government, unfolded over the course of eight hours at the Center for Court Innovation's headquarters in midtown Manhattan. As is typical of events that bring together experts from different disciplines and different parts of the country, consensus proved elusive. Nor is it possible to reduce the conversation to a handful of simple answers—the causes of any individual failure are too complex and idiosyncratic to yield easy generalizations. Context matters. What works in one setting might prove disastrous in another—and vice versa.

For all of these caveats, the roundtable did unearth a rich array of perspectives about the subject of failure. The edited transcript that follows has been organized into five subject areas, based on the topics that generated the most intense conversation over the course of the day-long roundtable.

Promoting Self-Reflection

The participants in the roundtable talked at length about how to balance two competing values of vital importance to successful criminal justice innovators: self-examination and relentless determination. Liz Glazer of the Westchester County District Attorney's Office started the day by talking about her desire to encourage criminal justice actors to be more thoughtful and to use data when identifying priorities and crafting policy. While other roundtable participants acknowledged the desirability of this as an aspirational goal, they also highlighted the real-life difficulties that prevent most criminal justice officials from realizing it, including the daily pressures of managing large bureaucracies, a cultural suspicion of anything "academic," and the need to achieve visible results in order to meet the demands of the public, the media and political officials. Often, innovators find they must sacrifice introspection in order to aggressively market their ideas and galvanize crucial allies. As one participant noted, "the only time real change occurs is when there is a maniac on a mission."

Getting the Right People to the Table

The question of how inclusive to be during the planning of a new project generated significant debate among roundtable participants. Some participants, including Jo-Ann Wallace of the National Legal Aid and Defenders Association, argued forcefully in favor of broadening the representation at the table, highlighting the value of two often-overlooked groups in particular: local residents and rank-and-file criminal justice staff. In making their case, these participants pointed to failures that stemmed from agency leaders formulating decisions in a vacuum, without relevant information that could be provided by outside parties. In response, several other roundtable participants, most notably Ron Corbett of the Massachusetts Supreme Court, talked about the dangers of being over-inclusive. They pointed out that the larger the group, the more difficult consensus is to achieve. Other participants noted that every voice is not created equal—often, it is only budget officials and political leaders (elected prosecutors, mayors, chief judges) who wield the necessary authority to make change happen.

Defining Success, Recognizing Failure

One of the principal challenges standing in the way of successful reform efforts that the group identified was the "win-lose" nature of much of what goes on within the criminal justice system. Put simply, the players that comprise the system (prosecutors, police, judges, probation, defense attorneys, corrections officials, pre-trial service agencies and others) often have competing agendas. As Michael Jacobson of the Vera Institute of Justice noted, "Failure depends upon where you stand." While all of the various agencies might agree on broad goals like reducing crime or promoting fairness, once the conversation moves to concrete strategies to achieve these goals, the consensus quickly evaporates. Phil Messer, the chief of police in Mansfield, Ohio, highlighted this reality when he talked about how a police success (making more drug arrests) was viewed as a failure by prosecutors, who struggled to handle the new cases flooding their dockets.

Identifying Specific Examples

As facilitator of the roundtable, Frank Hartmann made a deliberate effort to push participants to go beyond bland platitudes and banal generalities. In general, the participants in the conversation rose to the challenge, talking frankly about specific examples of failures that they had been involved with either directly or indirectly. These included reforms designed to link prostitutes to long-term drug treatment, to improve the processing of felony cases, and to enhance probation supervision of offenders. Implicit in this part of the conversation is the idea that it is possible to survive failure. No career can survive a steady diet of failure, of course. But the participants in the roundtable—each of whom has risen to a position of prominence in their chosen profession—are living testimony that failed experiments do not always lead to ruin.

Learning Lessons

At the end of the day's conversation, participants attempted to distill their experience into pragmatic advice for would-be innovators. Tim Murray of the Pre-Trial Services Resource Center summarized the feelings of many when he said, "I disagree and agree with almost everything that's been said [today] because there is no universal truth in this business." While the roundtable did not produce any universal truths, it did highlight several distinct tensions that have to be managed thoughtfully. These include the tension between a top-down and a bottom-up approach to change, between an inclusive approach to planning and one that emphasizes the use of "small platoons" of like-minded people, between engaging in self-reflection and being a cheerleader for reform, and between how success is defined for the criminal justice system and how it is defined for the individual agencies that comprise the system. While the answers will vary from place to place and project to project, few innovators can avoid having to make thoughtful choices among these options.

Building on these themes, what follows are selected highlights from the Center for Court Innovation and the Bureau of Justice Assistance's round-table conversation about failure and criminal justice reform.

Participants

Greg Berman, Director, Center for Court Innovation

Theron L. Bowman, Chief of Police, Arlington, Texas

Foster Cook, Director, TASC and Community Corrections, Jefferson County, Alabama

Ronald P. Corbett, Executive Director, Supreme Court of Massachusetts

Elizabeth Glazer, Deputy District Attorney, Westchester County, New York

Frank Hartmann (facilitator), Senior Research Fellow, John F. Kennedy School of Government, Harvard University

Domingo Herraiz, Director, U.S. Department of Justice, Bureau of Justice Assistance

Michael Jacobson, Director, Vera Institute of Justice

Hon. Robert G.M. Keating, Dean, New York State Judicial Institute

Adam Mansky, Director of Operations, Center for Court Innovation

Philip Messer, Chief of Police, Mansfield, Ohio

Timothy Murray, Director, Pre-Trial Services Resource Center

Hon. Juanita Newton, Administrative Judge, New York City Criminal Court

Kim Norris, Senior Policy Advisor, Bureau of Justice Assistance

Chauncey Parker, Commissioner, New York State Division of Criminal Justice Services

Michael Schrunk, District Attorney, Multnomah County, Oregon

Jo-Ann Wallace, President, National Legal Aid and Defenders Association

Alfred Siegel, Deputy Director, Center for Court Innovation

Promoting Self-Reflection

Hartmann: Let's begin by talking about a common tension faced by many innovators between the need for relentless determination and the need to occasionally pause and reflect to make sure the ship is pointed in the right direction. How do you achieve the proper balance?

Glazer: I have an example of this tension—and a potential failure—that I want to tell the group about. I want to preface it by saying that law enforcement agencies are under enormous pressure to live in the moment. Whenever something horrible happens, whenever there is a murder for example, there has to be an arrest. That is a demand that is rightly made by neighborhoods that are plagued by crime. Along with a need for constant action, I think there is also a real suspicion within many law enforcement agencies of reflection, of academia, of gathering statistics. The word "planning" can make people run screaming from the room. In Westchester, we have a single prosecuting authority but we have 43 police departments. The district attorney I work for is newly elected. So there is a real opportunity as she comes in to reorganize how things are done and to work with all 43 police departments collectively to solve the county's crime problems. But in order to do that, we actually have to know what the problems are. And in order to know what the problems are, you have to check the data. At this point, I've lost a lot of my audience of chiefs and commissioners, who are not terribly interested in planning. I think if you can show that gathering data helps solve crime in the here and now, then you can buy yourself time to have a real planning process. For me, this is an example of the kind of tension that Frank mentioned. In the law enforcement community, we always have to do something right now, but we don't always know enough to do something right now.

Corbett: I think we need to acknowledge that there is a degree of cultural suspicion of academics by practitioners and vice-versa. I remember 15 years ago talking with other probation executives about how little practice was informed by any of the readily available academic resources—and I don't think things have changed very much since then. There was almost a complete disconnect between practice and the parallel universe of research.

Siegel: It reminds me of when I was at the New York City Department of Probation. We tried to make the argument that if the City would make a modest investment in probation, the savings would be enormous to other parts of the system. We thought that was a very persuasive argument, but it never prevailed. You need a commitment from the powers that be and we didn't have enough juice to secure it. I think many initiatives die because they're the beneficiaries of lip service from the top rather than a genuine commitment.

Keating: The probation department in New York has had a lot of innovative ideas over the last decade—most of which have gone no place. My own perception of that agency is that it is pretty much politically powerless.

Jacobson: You really can't talk about any of this stuff outside the political context. That is how success or failure happens. I don't think there is a lot of tolerance for failure in government, certainly not at the executive levels, because you can't take the politics out of the stuff. I don't think there is a lot of self-reflection. In general, if your plan fails, you are done. It's very tough to reconcile the highfalutin' rhetoric that we're using here today around failure with the practical, political, budget-driven reality of government. I think Liz's project to convene the police chiefs in Westchester is doomed to failure. If the goal is to create some sort of seamless web of communication, that is just not going to happen. I don't think the DA's moral authority alone is enough to get 43 police chiefs on the same page. It's simple math. If you are trying to do some big thing with 43 different entities, whatever it is, it's not going to happen equally across all 43.

Cook: One of the challenges that I think Liz faces is that it is enormously difficult to build momentum for reform absent an immediate crisis. How do we improve the system without massive public support for dramatic change? It's like judges trying to improve the number of trials that are conducted. It's a wonderful goal. But no one much cares about it other than judges and attorneys. The public certainly doesn't—absent some horrific incident where a defendant is released because he or she was not tried in time.

Hartmann: So Liz is doomed to fail?

Cook: No, she is not going to fail because the process of getting the police together with the DA on a regular basis and pushing towards a common goal will have an incremental positive benefit in the long run, but perhaps not the immediate, huge benefit we'd all like to see.

Murray: When you are charging up the hill, do you ever really have time to stop and say, "Hey, am I going in the right direction?" In my limited experience, the answer is no. Say I've managed to convince a whole bunch of people to take a risk with me, to charge up the hill. The second I say, "Gee, I don't know, are we doing the right thing?" is when I lose all of them. And I don't just lose all of them just for that initiative, I lose all of them for the rest of my professional life.

Mansky: Tim hits the nail on the head. When you are trying to make the case for reform, to marshal your forces, you want to put your initiative in the best possible light. You want to show that your new program will work. But I think that often comes at the expense of self-reflection and continuing to improve. I don't think any of us want to end up being cheerleaders with no credibility.

Schrunk: How do you create the space for self-reflection? As a newly elected DA, I quickly discovered that before I started any project that I had to plan in advance for some early wins. You've got to market change. I found it enormously helpful to pick off low-hanging fruit and have some short-term successes that would help me build toward the larger, ultimate goal. You have to feed the beast. You have to show the public, the elected officials, your key constituents, that you are making progress. Otherwise, they won't have the patience to help you reach your ultimate goal. And if you get one or two of Liz's 43 police chiefs to have some immediate success, other people are going to look at it and say I want to be part of that success.

Getting the Right People to the Table

Wallace: I would argue that you increase the likelihood of failure if you don't have the right people around the table. You could have the right goal, but if everyone who needs to be there to address the goal isn't at the table in the planning stages, then you can still fail. And often we don't make a place at the table for the people from the community in which the problem lies. As an example, in Washington DC, we had to really battle to get some community representatives on our local criminal justice coordinating commission. When the commission looked at escapes from a local halfway house, the community representatives brought a unique perspective to this conversation. They said to all of the criminal justice agencies at the table, "Wait a minute, have you ever stepped foot in the halfway house?" They identified a number of concrete reasons that may have contributed to people leaving. For example, for the first three days of residency, you have to stay in the house. So if you have a job, you just lost your job. Without the voice of the community, I don't think that the response of the commission would have ended up being as effective.

Glazer: I think we sometimes make a fetish of getting a lot of people around the table and then the problem is, okay, now we're all around the table what do we do? The goal has to be incredibly concrete and every person has to have a self-interested reason why they're around the table.

Jacobson: Sometimes, the only way to overcome the system's inertia and the self-interest of all the parties is not by getting people to come to the table. It's by hammering people essentially into submission.

Corbett: I think there are myths about how to achieve change. I would propose that one of the myths is that you have to have the right people at the table.

Hartmann: Why do you think this isn't really important?

Corbett: Because you can't get the big elephants in line easily. And you'll wear yourself out trying. Success is often a zero sum game. Success for one agency will inevitably be a loss for another. In my 33 years, I've never seen real change come about from getting everyone at the table. Every time you add another big agency to your planning effort, the difficulty of getting people to agree and coordinate goes up geometrically. So as a result you are doomed before you start.

Hartmann: Tell us the opposite way to proceed.

Corbett: Little platoons. You bite off a small piece of this giant system and go after people that you know have both the will and the political power to make change happen. You find little corners of entities—what some have called "skunk works"—and you find staff with energy and ambition and talent. You experiment at the margins. You come out with a little product like one drug court in the corner of the state rather than trying to get the entire statewide judicial infrastructure to agree they want to move forward with a specific solution. You get that first drug court and then you tinker with it. When it succeeds, all of a sudden one thing leads to two, leads to four, leads to ten.

Jacobson: There are a lot of ways to do systematic change. I think you can do it by getting everyone at the table. Although I'm pretty cynical myself about that approach, especially as a former budget official. As a budget official, to be totally honest, I was able to get a lot done with absolutely nobody at the table.

Glazer: I'm with Ron Corbett 100 percent. He is absolutely right as far as the little platoon. From the example we started with, I can tell you that with 43 police chiefs, it is like herding cats. You can't do it. When you have a multitude of people at the table, it's usually a disaster. But I think you can start with a small group of like-minded people and build up some momentum and hopefully attract the rest to join you. At the end of the day, everything is personal. There's nothing wrong with jump-starting the process by working with people who you already have a good relationship with for one reason or another. Sometimes you have to kind of dip your toes in the water before you take the plunge.

Keating: Often the best ideas fail because we have not gotten buy-in from the people that do the work. In the past, some great ideas have died a still-born death because line staff would hear about them and say one of two things: "(A) we don't think that is a great idea so we're not going to do it. Or (B), we know if we stall, there will be another commissioner and he will have a whole new set of ideas." For me, it always comes back to trying to figure out what is in it for the people that do the work. How are we going to improve the quality of their workday? Unfortunately, a lot of times the new ideas we come up with create more work for people. And when you're presenting that, when you're standing in front of a probation officer for example with these great ideas and they say, "You're telling me now I have to go to court more often or write more reports and I have to see probationers much more frequently? It's much easier for me to violate people and run to court and drop it in the judge's hands than to spend a lot of time working with people who are failures." Often, what looks like programmatic failure is really a crisis of marketing.

Messer: One of the underlying themes to the conversation so far is the importance of communication. Often we fail to communicate with the troops in the trenches about what we're doing and why we need to do it. When we have looked at our failures, when we trace them back, we often find a gap in communication between leadership and the people actually charged with doing the work. And the feedback we get from the folks on the frontlines is that, "If we had understood why you were doing this, we could have probably done things more efficiently."

Corbett: The top-down model of change is more difficult than bottom up change. For me, a better way to go is to catch some of your best line people doing something right, to go around your organization looking for innovation at the street level. Shine a light on it. Reinforce it. Take those people and move them around the organization, give them a lot of credit. At the end of the day, you will have an innovation that has street credibility because it has already been practiced. Peter Drucker once said, "The only time real change occurs is when there is a maniac on a mission," and I believe that.

Schrunk: I love people who want to do the right thing for the right reason. I call them do-righters. I also have learned that sometimes people want to do the right thing for the wrong reason. The wrong reason could be there is a pot of money to be divided. It could be the desire for a front-page headline. It could be a commissioner needs an issue to get elected or even a DA is on a crusade to be a congressman. So I think we need to figure out what buttons are going to bring people in.

Corbett: This leads me to another myth. And that is that people are interested in positive change. By and large, this is simply not true. In general, when you introduce the notion that criminal justice agencies ought to change the way they do things, this is treated as a toxin rather than a wonderful opportunity to move things forward.

Murray: I feel very conflicted listening to you guys. I disagree and agree with almost everything that's been said because there is no universal truth in this business. I think people who are good at making change—systemic or otherwise, because sometimes you can pull off larger reform—these folks have a gift for figuring out who they need at the table and how to convince them that change is in their interest. And folks, if I can't do that, I don't have an idea that is going to work. The trick is to manage all of this without selling my soul. I can't say "Oh no, so-and-so is not on board unless I wear shorts.... Okay, everybody go change into your shorts." And then all of a sudden you don't remember what the initial idea was. That is flat out failure too.

Defining Success, Recognizing Failure

Parker: What we often fail to do in government is to identify very clearly what the goal is. And for us in criminal justice, the goal is simple: to reduce crime. When you start talking about sharing information, why is that important? Well, that will reduce crime. Just connect the dots. Why should we collect DNA in a timely fashion? Because it can reduce crime. Everything has to be explained in terms of a clear goal, which we all share.

Corbett: I'm not sure most criminal justice agencies can even recognize failure, let alone understand it. It is not my impression that most criminal justice leaders walk around having a clear notion in their mind as to whether they're succeeding or failing, other than in the most gross ways: "Is the newspaper running me down? Am I about to be indicted? Is the money missing?" That is not what we're talking about here today. Can we even recognize failure when it occurs so we can come to understand it? Maybe I'm wrong, but I don't think it's common for any branch of criminal justice to engage in any routine way in after-action analysis. The U.S. Army model is that when something doesn't work the way you want it to, you should spend a little bit of time unpacking that so as to understand it and not repeat the same thing.

Hartmann: Any reactions to Ron's point about the inability to recognize failure?

Schrunk: One challenge is that it's often difficult to recognize that within successes there are failures. We may have taken the hill, but we paid a horrible price climbing it.

Messer: For us police chiefs, to recognize failure is not too difficult: we look at crime rates. The challenge is that law enforcement is often quick to blame others for their failures. It's easy to say, "The prosecutor dealt the case away. Or the judge let too many people out. Or the probation department failed." As a police chief I can recognize failure based on what is occurring in my city. But if we're not happy with the answer, people are pretty quick to say, "Okay, now whose fault is this?"

Schrunk: What this highlights for me is the dynamic tension that exists between system success and the success of individual agencies. It's one thing to articulate clear goals and clear messages about improving the system of justice or reducing crime or what have you. But once you get past broad, systemic goals to actually come up with real, concrete strategies, you often find that my success is your failure. For example, if pretrial services succeeds in getting more people out of jail, they might define that as a success, whereas the local police force or prosecutor might not see that as being in their interest. So the tension that exists across roles when you are trying to do system-level improvements is really palpable. It is very difficult to get everybody at the table to agree on specific strategies, because a lot of times they see it as, "If you win, then I lose."

Bowman: Mike Schrunk is absolutely correct. I believe that there are two sometimes conflicting goals. One is reducing crime and the other is the administration of justice. And unless we resolve these conflicting goals, we're going to continue to fail as a system. We call this a system, but of course there is no individual point of accountability for the entire system.

Jacobson: Failure depends upon where you stand. I think of the issue of technical parole violations. To me those are failures, but if you ask parole officials they will say, "No, that is a success. We caught that guy before he was going down a slippery slope and slammed him back into prison." Not a speck of research says this is even remotely true. Take a place like California. There are 120,000 people on parole in California and each year they send back 70,000 for technical violations. They go back for an average of two and a half months at a total cost of almost a billion dollars. So you ask someone like me, and I say, who would spend a billion dollars sending 70,000 people back to prison for three months? Who could possibly say that if we have a billion dollars to spend on law enforcement, what we want to do is catch 70,000 parolees after they test positive for drugs and slam them back into prison for two and a half months? But for parole officials in California, it's a success. You are getting people off your caseload. You're doing good law enforcement work. And you are minimizing your political risk. Meanwhile, the corrections people go berserk, because they have to spend a billion dollars on technical violators. The issue of whether that is a success or failure, is a really interesting, very highly politically loaded question.

Schrunk: I think of the young men and women that I hire, they want to slug felons. They want to put notches on their belts. They want to get the maximum punishment. It doesn't matter whether it's for a misdemeanor or property crime or violent crime. They view that as a success. I think that is wrong. So our individuals, we have a whole bunch of agencies that have individual criteria for success. Sometimes I think taken together, they contribute to overall failure.

Parker: We are paid by tax payers to reduce crime. We're all in the public safety business. Although it's a challenge, when we work together, crime is going to go down. Where is it written that everyone gets to set their own goals? At the New York State Division of Criminal Justice Services, we made it a condition of all of our grants that you have to share information across agency lines. That is now a condition of funding. If you don't do it, you will lose your funding.

Corbett: Apart from the police, I don't think the rest of us have been very good about specifying what it is we are trying to achieve, and the failure to do that makes it difficult to recognize either success or failure.

Newton: If you said to me, is the criminal court of the City of New York working? I would say, yes. We resolve cases and controversies and we do that well. But I think the public has a very different set of expectations about what they want courts to do. If you speak to the administrators and judges, they would say, yes, we are meeting our mandate, but the public perception might be very different.

Wallace: I actually think that in many instances the public has a greater understanding that failure is a part of success than we do. For example, from the drug court experience we learned that relapse is often a part of rehabilitation for drug addicts. We had to do a lot of work to train prosecutors, judges, defense attorneys to accept the reality of relapse, but a lot of the general public already knows this intuitively because they've seen their sons or daughters or cousins go through treatment and recovery.

Fuster: In Puerto Rico, we have had a drug court for 12 years now. At the beginning it was only one district, now it's in every district. And it would appear that they're very successful. Those that graduate from the drug court program have a low recidivism rate. But only 25 percent of all of those that could have gone through the drug court got to the drug court. So the recidivism is very, very low, but maybe those guys were going to behave anyway, with or without the drug court.

Messer: With drug courts, the fear of failure is almost corrupting the process. Sure, there's a high success rate. But I can remember asking why don't you take this guy or that guy into drug court? The answer was, "No way. We don't think that guy is going to make it and we don't want him showing up on our stats."

Hartmann: I want to come back to this issue that a win for you is a loss for me. What happens if Phil Messer arrests a bunch of people and shoves them into the court system. That's a win for him, he looks good. But all of a sudden the media is all over the court and the prosecutor for not moving the cases fast enough.

Messer: We see it all the time in Ohio. I have a drug task force that I oversee. We have been very successful in making more arrests. But the second we do this, my phone starts ringing off the hook from local prosecutors who say, "What are you doing? Slow down on your arrests because the system can't handle it." Conversely, the court's success could be my failure. If we're not arresting people the way we should, the courts are able to keep up with their dockets, they're able to move cases on time. So there has to be a balance.

Cook: I can think of a couple of other examples, mainly prison and jail over-crowding. In our state right now we are working to reduce overcrowding, but at the same time, we have some real public safety problems that need to be addressed. Our police chiefs are under a lot of pressure because of spiraling murder rates. So part of the system is busy working on how to get people out of jail and prison and back into the community faster. And there are plenty of communities that are not really interested in accepting these people back on their streets. So there is a lot of tension between the effort to solve prison overcrowding and local communities concerned about crime.

Murray: When you talk about judging the success or failure of new pro-grams, you have to acknowledge that the status quo is not in fact a success. When you introduce a reform, the grading system is always applied to the innovation, but it's never applied to the status quo. The status quo is not something I would want anyone to aspire to.

Keating: The manifest failure of the status quo helps make the case for change a lot easier. When we first started the Midtown Community Court, we based it on the fact that virtually any new way of doing business would have been better than the standard operating practice at that time. The criminal courts were dismissing 55 percent of the cases and no one was going to jail. So the standard we used as our argument to do something dif-ferent was the total bankruptcy of the system that was presently operating.

Murray: Usually change is being introduced to something that is already failing. In fact, because it's failing, you are trying in your own humble way to offer some kind of remedy. Because of this, you are put under the micro-scope, as you should be, to see if this change makes things better or worse. I remember testifying before Congress and somebody asking me, "Would an appropriate measure of the effectiveness of drug court be to follow people around for seven years after they graduated and then have them pee in a cup and run a records check?" I said that was an absolutely exquisite stan-dard, but then let's do the same thing with people released from prison and then we get to compare.

Identifying Specific Examples

Hartmann: What I would really like to hear now from you are specific ex-amples of failures that you've either seen or been part of first-hand. I think it is important to send the message that it is often possible to fail and still survive to fight another day, provided you learn the right lessons.

Keating: This goes back some time, but at one point we were trying to do nighttime jury trials in felony cases in Brooklyn. This was an answer to a specific problem—we were having trouble getting defendants to trial in a timely fashion. And we thought if we did trials at night, there would be fewer distractions for the judges and it would be more convenient for witnesses to testify. We did the project for about a year and a half, maybe two years. And as it turned out we did try cases much more expeditiously. However, everybody involved in the system hated it. The lawyers hated it. The jurors hated it. Even the complainants whom we thought would benefit the most didn't like it. The only one who liked it was me, and of course I took great delight in saying this is a success, why doesn't anyone agree with me? In the final analysis, we had not done enough talking to the attorneys. What we all forgot, was that most criminal attorneys do their office work between 4pm and 7pm. That is when they see clients. That is when they prepare for their other trials. So this added responsibility was not such a great idea from their perspective. On reflection, we didn't really talk to the people seriously.

Newton: I want to share a failure of my own. Many years ago the courts in New York came under court order to reduce the arrest-to-arraignment time to under 24 hours. Judge Keating, who oversaw the criminal courts at the time, was able to take the average from five days to 24 hours. So when I inherited the job a few years later, I decided that I would try to take it a step further by saying we no longer want to achieve an average of 24 hours but rather we want to ensure that every individual defendant is arraigned within 24 hours. Well, talk about an idea that went over like a lead balloon. People told me flat out, "It's too much to do. We're already doing some good and we don't want to do any more good." I was totally taken by surprise. We had the right people in the room. We had a financial incentive, because if we don't meet the court-imposed mandate, there are tremendous fines. Moreover, if we end up having to release people on the streets, it's a public safety issue. But it was a poorly conceived plan.

Murray: Sometimes you can pull the plug too early. I had a program in Miami. After the initial success of the drug court, law enforcement came to us and said, "You know, along a particular roadway in Miami, all of the prostitutes that we pick up have drug paraphernalia. Why don't you do something about it?" We said, absolutely. And so we started a new program. We took in 60 women, and 60 women absconded. That is failure. It scared us to our toes. We worried this failure would have a ripple effect on all of the other efforts underway to promote drug treatment within the justice system. So we chickened out. We pulled the plug. I think any time you pull the plug on a program, successful or failed, without taking the opportunity to see what was learned, you botched the job. We went back and found those women a year or so later and discovered that many of them had children, which ultimately was the cause of the failure of that program. They had children, and we were putting them in residential environments or therapeutic communities, which often required them to leave their children. So their fear of leaving their children and government getting its hooks on their kids was a totally understandable fear and one that we could have programmed for if we had more awareness of what was being taught to us. So the real failure wasn't that 60 women absconded. The real failure was that we were so shocked by it, that we shut the program down and didn't use it as a learning opportunity.

Siegel: In New York City, there are something like 60,000 probationers. Someone is on felony probation for five years, and for the last three of those years, probation supervision is not terribly onerous. When I was at probation, we hoped they didn't re-offend, but if they didn't, it wasn't because we were doing anything affirmative to make that happen. Given this, we thought that we should find a way to move them off probation supervision earlier so that we could spend more time with people who we knew were more likely to fail, because the research, such as it was, very clearly stated that most people who fail do so within the first six months to a year. But the resistance to this idea was uniform. Politicians opposed it. Judges didn't want to sign off on early discharge applications. We wanted to do a better job with those probationers that we could influence, and nobody was interested. So I think sometimes failure is a product of the inability to articulate an argument and to marshal the right constituents to get behind it.

Jacobson: When I started in the budget office, I wanted to speed up the processing of felony cases in New York City, which is an incredibly mundane goal. I can tell you first-hand that no one cares about it. And the reason I was so interested in it was that there are thousands of people who are stuck on Rikers Island simply because it is taking an excessive amount of time to process their cases. I thought that if we could speed up the process, then we could save literally hundreds of millions of dollars in incarceration costs, and that the mayor could take that money and put it in early childhood education. It just makes you cry, it's all so beautiful. But we couldn't do it because everyone was so invested in delay. It works for everyone. The prosecutors loved it. Judges didn't mind it. No one thought it was a particular problem and as much as we tried to push on all of those parties, to tell them that it was actually in their self interest to do this, or simply to bribe them, nothing worked.

Wallace: When I was at the public defenders' service in Washington DC, I came to the conclusion that we were devoting the lion's share of our resources to felony cases at the expense of working with juveniles. Research tells us that is upside down. Prevention is critical. Many public defender offices train people by putting them in juvenile court first and then letting people work their way up to handling serious felonies. Our juveniles were suffering to some degree because people weren't staying in the juvenile court long enough to understand how kids think and the difference between children and adults. So my goal was to create a unit with special training for lawyers and wrap-around services for juveniles. Anyway, long story short, when I made the decision to leave the defenders office, the initiative just stopped.

Cook: Back in the early '90s, a friend of mine authored a piece of legislation called the Mandatory Drug Treatment Act. In the process of signing up sponsors, we went to the administrative office of the courts. They agreed to sign on because they saw the bill as a vehicle for authorizing DUI schools. Thanks to their support, the legislation passed. It enabled folks around the state to set up DUI schools, which use the leverage of the criminal justice system to get people to pay them lots of money. The original intent—to promote the use of treatment—was never realized. It goes to show you how a good idea in the hands of a naïve innovator can go wrong. We were naïve about the politics.

Murray: There is another kind of failure that's worth talking about and that is when reforms ultimately become the very thing they sought to reform.

Hartmann: Give us an example.

Murray: Drug courts. Drug courts have gotten so rigid in some places and so committed to maintaining an artificially high success rate. Bail reports are another great example. For many years, people were held in jail pending trial, despite the presumption of innocence, only because they didn't have money in their pocket to pay bail. Not so long ago, some people got together to reform that. Let's collect information, do risk assessments, suggest ways to manage risk and give that to decision makers. Great. That is a reform, that is a fix. That is a success. Then over time as these programs get embedded more and more in the status quo, success becomes defined not by how many people get released but on the size of the agency budget. And success gets defined by the ability to stay out of the public view, to avoid controversy. And pretty soon, I tend to become more and more chicken, and then pretty soon I don't recommend any one for release.

Learning Lessons

Hartmann: We've talked about some examples of failure. In the time we have left, I want to focus our attention on the lessons. Imagine that your brother or your sister who is 15 years younger than you was going into this business—what advice would you give them?

Keating: When you are dealing with reforming large institutions in the criminal justice system, sometimes you need large people. You can talk about doing a platoon and all of this other stuff at the margins, but unless you have a mayor or a chief judge or someone with an enormous amount of political capital who is willing to go out and embarrass other people, change will not occur.

Corbett: I don't know if you know a book called "Street Level Bureaucracy," but it argues that all public sector organizations are really run by line staff. Don't fool yourself that you can run a public sector organization from the top.

Bowman: I agree the rank and file have to be on board but sometimes the top has to show leadership. The rank and file are not always in a position to fully understand the program or potential results. But the rank and file, if not brought on board, can kill an otherwise good program with good potential. So I think it's important that if you are introducing a new innovation to maybe go with the early innovators, those few key people who are willing to take a risk. And that buys you time to bring the rest of the rank and file into the picture.

Murray: One of the lessons that I have learned, first and foremost, is that the criminal justice system is a monster and it has an amazing ability to regain whatever shape and behaviors it had before you started poking at it. So if anything, you never achieve the change you intended, and it's unrealistic to expect to. But that can't deter you from tilting at the windmills.

Jacobson: Failure may be important to the natural process where you learn and eventually get to success. But that does not comport easily with the trend in government to get more and more specific about measurement and deliverables. Many government funding contracts are now performance-based and they're very specific. I yearn for the good old days where government could just dispense a bucket of cash, but those days are over. Today, there is less and less wiggle room. No one wants to give taxpayers' money out to just anyone or to tolerate cruddy performance. Even if you can get a government official to understand that you are dealing with a complicated problem and you are making progress, if you aren't meeting your deliverables, forget about it. So if we want to understand failure and promote innovation, I think we need to get to a place where contracts do have concrete goals, but they aren't set in stone and there is some flexibility on the part of government. This is easy to say and hard to do.

Norris: What this really underlines for me is the value of trust. I think you need to develop trust with your partners—and with your funders. Trust is the only thing that can help you weather small failures along the way.

Berman: As the leader of a non-profit organization, I often feel like a professional supplicant. The truth of the matter is that the typical non-profit has next to no power. We always need someone else, usually in government, to authorize and pay for our work. We can't do anything without permission. And in my experience, it usually isn't possible to get that permission without over-promising what you will deliver. So my question is, is it possible to generate the political will and momentum for reform without having to overestimate the number of people you're going to serve or the impact that your initiative will have? Can we introduce some realism into the process?

Bowman: If we're going to have an impact ultimately on encouraging change and innovation and tolerance of failure, I think we have to convince the general public, because they are the ones who put pressure on me when things don't work. Several people have raised the issue of fear of failure. I think you need to really understand the sources of that fear. And I believe that fear of failure is not driven internally, it's imposed externally from the folks who put us where we are. I don't lose sleep at night worrying that the crime rate is up one point or two points above where it should be. My stress comes from the authorizing environment, the citizens. If you can persuade them, then you can get me to implement whatever change is necessary. I've heard it said that change only occurs when the pain of the status quo exceeds the pain of reform.

Schrunk: I came across an article in a business magazine recently and it was talking about corporate managers promising less than they knew they would produce—they would deliberately underestimate to ensure that they didn't fail. I think this is good advice, but at the same time we all know that in order to get funding, we often have to promise that we're going to save the free world. That is a dilemma we all face.

Siegel: We're all in the business of taking risks. The question is, where do you go after you take the risk and failed? Do you have the guts to do it again? People don't like to admit failure. When you admit failure, it puts you at a disadvantage when you go to get funding or get the support you need.

Corbett: Surviving failure is crucial. At the end of the day, our job is to try stuff. If it doesn't work, try to fix it and roll it out again. If that doesn't work, try something else.

Newton: I think it is important to remember why we are doing this in the first place. What keeps us coming back to the job is that we have this notion of justice that we think is critical. Earlier today, Ron Corbett mentioned the idea of "maniacs on a mission." I'd like to think that the maniacs are still going to keep coming up with new ways to improve the system because it's the right thing to do.

9 Try Again, Fail Again, Fail Better

This is a lightly edited version of a speech delivered at the National Institute of Justice in Washington, D.C. in April 2011.

It is going to be enormously difficult for me to live up to the title of this lecture series, "Research for the Real World."

First of all, I'm not a researcher. In fact, I'm not really a numbers person.

I'm also not a criminal justice practitioner, not in any real sense of the word. I've never arrested anybody. I've never prosecuted a case. I've never supervised anyone on probation.

Given all this, you may be asking yourself, "Why did John Laub and the National Institute of Justice make this invitation?" I think I was invited because I've written a couple of books about criminal justice reform. In doing so, there are two lenses that I sought to bring to the topic of criminal justice reform. One is the perspective of the professional amateur, the person who feels the freedom, perhaps through ignorance, to ask the simple question. The second lens I bring to the table is that I think of myself as a writer. And like a lot of writers, I tend to think in three-act structures—beginning, middle, and end.

So my remarks today have a three-act structure. First, I want to talk a little bit about the agency that I run, the Center for Court Innovation, because I think it will help clarify my perspective on criminal justice. Then I want to drill down a little deeper and talk about one of the reforms that we've been responsible for implementing, which is the community court model. And then finally, I want to offer some lessons that I've learned about program implementation, both from my direct experience helping to create nearly two dozen demonstration projects in New York but also from the process of writing *Trial and Error in Criminal Justice Reform* with Aubrey Fox.

What is the Center for Court Innovation? The Center is a not-for-profit organization that has managed to forge a unique relationship with the New York State court system, which, in essence, hires us to function as their R&D arm. This arrangement is the product of three remarkably talented people: New York State Chief Judge Jonathan Lippman, former New York State Chief Judge Judith Kaye, and my predecessor as the executive director of the Center for Court Innovation, John Feinblatt. The original vision for the Center was that the court system would authorize us not just to study difficult problems within the justice system, but to devise new solutions and then implement them.

While our home is in New York, we have always sought to reach beyond the five boroughs. We've aggressively tried to disseminate what we've done in New York and help other reformers around the world learn from our experiments. The Department of Justice, and the Bureau of Justice Assistance in particular, has been our partner in much of this work.

What the Center for Court Innovation is trying to do in broad strokes is to reform the criminal justice system. I think that there are probably dozens of ways one could go about reforming the criminal justice system. There's impact litigation. There's lobbying. There's public advocacy. Our model is a little bit different. What we're trying to do is to reform the criminal justice system by working in close partnership with government to change practice on the ground.

Broadly speaking, we have three core areas of business. The first is research. We have a deep commitment to data and analysis. We study problems from a variety of different angles. For example, right now we're digging into the neighborhood of Brownsville. Brownsville is a community in Brooklyn that last year was, on a per capita basis, the most violent neighborhood in New York City. We're looking at court and police statistics, but we're also going out into the neighborhood and interviewing influential members of the community. We're conducting focus groups. We're surveying local residents and asking them what they think about their neighborhood and about the justice system. When we do this kind of work, our purpose is not just knowledge for knowledge's sake, but rather we're doing research to inform the development of demonstration projects.

Our goal in creating demonstration projects is to field-test new ideas and to show new thinking in action. Since we started, we've developed nearly two dozen different demonstration projects in New York. Some of them are big; some of them are small. Some of them deal with serious felony-level cases; some of them deal with minor infractions. Some of them deal with adults; some of them deal with juveniles. But the theme that weaves through them all is a desire to push the justice system away from a rote, mechanistic approach to case processing and towards a more individualized approach that tries to solve the problems of individual defendants, victims, and neighborhoods.

All of our demonstration projects have researchers assigned to them, whether on a part-time or full-time basis, and our largest demonstration projects have been the subject of independent evaluations by researchers from the Urban Institute, John Jay College, and the National Center for State Courts.

After we have developed hands-on experience implementing a given demonstration project, we then go out to provide what we call "technical assistance" to the field. We're trying to aid justice reformers around the country, both inside and outside of government, helping them implement new solutions to local problems.

Our three core areas of business are meant to be mutually reinforcing. Research is the foundation upon which demonstration projects are built. In turn, our experience running real-life programs is what gives us the credibility to provide assistance to the field. And then what we learn from our engagement with the world we try to feed back into our demonstration projects so that we're a learning institution as well as a teaching institution.

One of the projects that we've been responsible for helping to create and promote over the last decade is the community court model. Community courts are incredibly complicated beasts, but if you boil them down to their essence, I think they're trying to achieve two basic goals.

The first goal is to take low-level offending seriously. Now, this emphasis on minor offending doesn't come out of nowhere. Rather, it's an acknowledgement of a simple fact. Despite what we see on TV, criminal courts in this country are not inundated with murder and rape cases. If you look at the statistics, more than 80 percent of the caseload in our criminal courts are misdemeanor offenses: shoplifting, vandalism, minor drug possession.[103] That's not where the focus is, but that's where the numbers are.

In addressing minor crime, community courts implicitly honor the idea of broken windows that was first advanced by George Kelling and James Wilson a generation ago.[104] So, first and foremost, what community courts are about is trying to strengthen the judicial response to minor crime and make sure that there are real consequences for behavior that erodes the quality of life in our neighborhoods.

The second goal that community courts are trying to achieve is to move the justice system away from using incarceration as a default sentence in responding to crime. Now, at first glance, these two goals might seem to be in conflict with one another. Broken windows enforcement typically is

---

[103] Robert C. LaFountain. "Examining the Work of State Courts: An Analysis of 2008 State Court Caseloads," *National Center for State Courts* (2008), p. 47.

[104] George L. Kelling and James Q. Wilson. "Broken Windows," *The Atlantic*, March 1, 1982.

about bringing more people into the system, while promoting alternatives to incarceration is logically about pushing people out of the system.

Community courts' solution to this dilemma is pretty straightforward: they provide judges with additional options, so that they don't have to choose between jail and nothing. This means creating community restitution projects that actually target hotspots and eyesores in the local community. And it means offering the kinds of social services, whether it be job training or mental health counseling or drug treatment, that might prevent someone from coming back to court again and again as a recidivist.

Inside the courtroom, community courts adopt a problem-solving orientation to address the underlying problems of defendants. Outside the courthouse, community courts strive to engage local residents in doing justice. This is based on a belief that true and enduring justice doesn't come from living in a police state. True and enduring justice comes when government and citizens work together in an atmosphere of mutual respect to promote pro-social values. And that's why community courts convene town hall meetings, organize neighborhood clean-ups, and host youth development programs.

Before I became the director of the Center for Court Innovation, I had the privilege of serving as the lead planner of the Red Hook Community Justice Center, a community court in southwest Brooklyn. I started working in Red Hook in the early 1990s, before New York had experienced the incredible public safety improvements that we've enjoyed over the last 15 years. What struck me about the neighborhood first and foremost was its geography. The physical distance between Red Hook and Wall Street is very, very small. It kind of feels like you could throw a rock from Red Hook and hit a banker on Wall Street.

The physical distance is small, but the psychological distance couldn't be more vast. Red Hook is traditionally a poor and working class neighborhood. It is home to one of New York's oldest and largest public housing developments. It is surrounded on three sides by water and cut off from the rest of Brooklyn by an elevated expressway. And it is a neighborhood that has a reputation for drugs and disorder. The low moment for Red Hook came in the early 1990s when an elementary school principal named Patrick Daly was killed in broad daylight when he left school to search for a student who was truant. He got caught in a crossfire between two rival drug dealers.

In the aftermath of this horrible event, the local district attorney, Charles J. Hynes, did two things. First, he said that his office was going to prosecute both drug dealers, even though they couldn't tell whose bullet had actually killed Patrick Daly. But the second thing he did was to state publicly that aggressive law enforcement wasn't going to change the dynamics in

Red Hook—something else was needed. He called for the creation of a community court in Red Hook. And that's when I came on board.

The Red Hook Community Justice Center opened in 2000, operating out of a renovated parochial school that had been vacant for 20 years and was a powerful symbol of the neighborhood's decline. Red Hook is an official branch of the New York State Court System with a real judge and attorneys that handle thousands of misdemeanor and low-level felony cases each year.

Red Hook is currently the subject of an NIJ-funded evaluation being conducted by the National Center for State Courts. While we wait for results from this study, researchers from the Center for Court Innovation are constantly examining the project to see how it's doing.

The numbers suggest that the project has changed sentencing practice, dramatically reducing the use of jail. At the same time, Red Hook has bolstered public trust in justice and improved defendant perceptions of fairness.

Each year, we host hundreds of visitors to Red Hook. Some end up replicating the community court model in full. And some come to look at just a piece of what we do. They are interested in how we do community service. They are interested in how we redesigned the courthouse to make it more user-friendly. Two out of three visitors who visit Red Hook say that they're going to implement something that they learned in Red Hook when they return home.

Now I want to pivot and talk not about content but about process, and in particular, I want to try to offer some lessons that I've learned not just from community courts, but from other criminal justice reform efforts around the country. These lessons are drawn from a multi-faceted inquiry into failed criminal justice reforms that we've undertaken over the last couple of years in concert with the Bureau of Justice Assistance.

This policy inquiry is based on a couple of operating assumptions. The first operating assumption, to paraphrase Teddy Roosevelt, is that failure is a fact of life, that there is no effort without error. And the second operating assumption, to paraphrase Abraham Lincoln, is that it's human nature not to want to talk about failure so much.

To be clear, when we talk "failure" in this context, we are not talking about errors of corruption or malfeasance or incompetence. Instead, we are talking about case studies where a bunch of dedicated people got together to try something difficult and fell short of their goals for one reason or another.

By shining a spotlight on this topic, we are trying to nudge criminal justice away from a culture of blame and fingerpointing when something goes wrong. Instead, we want to encourage the field of criminal justice to embrace innovation and honest self-reflection.

I think it probably goes without saying that some other fields are better at talking openly about failure than the criminal justice system is. For example, Eli Lilly, the pharmaceutical company, for many years hosted "failure parties" for their scientists when they had performed outstanding research—even if it hadn't led to any new products for the company.[105] I think it is fair to say that there are no failure parties in criminal justice.

In the spirit of honesty and humility, I want to offer nine lessons that I've learned about implementing new programs. As you will see, none of these lessons amount to rocket science, but I can tell you that even an agency like mine which is explicitly devoted to being thoughtful about innovation, has made these mistakes over and over again.

Lesson One: Not all failures are alike. There's a famous quote from Tolstoy that says that "happy families are all alike," but that "every unhappy family is unhappy in its own way."[106] I think that's probably true when it comes to criminal justice failure: each failure is the product of its own unique negative alchemy that involves local personalities and bad luck and a challenging environment.

Having said this, if you take a step back, there are four basic categories that failed criminal justice reform efforts seem to cluster into: *failure of concept*, when reformers just pursue the wrong ideas; *failure of implementation*, when reformers have the right idea, but they implement it poorly; *failure of marketing and politics*, when reformers are stymied by local politics and fail to win the resources, the manpower, or the money they need to move forward; and *failure of self-reflection*, when reformers are not thoughtful about documenting results or lack the capacity to respond to conditions on the ground as they change.

Lesson Two: Our expectations of criminal justice reform should be modest. I want to read two passages that I think speak to this lesson. The first is from a professor at Hamilton College, Paul Gary Wyckoff, who is the author of *Policy and Evidence in a Partisan Age*. In it, he writes:

> Government policy is consistently oversold, to citizens, to politicians, and even to academics. It is oversold by both conservatives and liberals, in different but curiously similar ways. Over and over, we elect officials in the naïve belief that they can pull some sort of magic lever to fix our social and economic problems. When that doesn't work, we "throw the bums out" and elect someone else to pull a different lever or even to pull the same lever in the opposite direction, but what many Americans don't understand, but empirical studies bear out, is that in many circumstances, the government levers are simply disconnected from the problems that

---

[105] Thomas M. Burton. "By Learning From Failures, Lilly Keeps Drug Pipeline Full," *The Wall Street Journal*, April 21, 2004.

[106] Leo Tolstoy. *Anna Karenina*. Penguin Classics, 2004, p. 1.

they are supposed to address.[107]

Wyckoff is talking about policy in general, but I think that lesson is equally applicable to the world of criminal justice.

This brings me to my second quote, which is from a professor at George Mason named David Wilson. Wilson writes, "Most criminal justice interventions only work with people for a short period of time. For example, a court-mandated batterer intervention program typically only involves about 28 contact hours. Changing behavior that has developed over a lifetime in just 28 hours is a tall order."[108]

The truth of the matter is that we rarely speak this kind of truth to those in power, whether they be government officials or elected officials or foundation officers. In fact, there's an enormous temptation to do the opposite—to exaggerate what you're going to achieve.

My father is a businessman, and he taught me that one of the core lessons of business is to underpromise and overdeliver. But we don't do that in criminal justice. We violate this lesson again and again and again.

The Center for Court Innovation is not immune to this phenomenon. Over the years, we have had a number of process evaluations performed of our own work. When we took a step back and analyzed what we had learned from these evaluations, the number one mistake that we made over and over again was overestimating the caseload volume of new projects during the planning process. I don't think we did this deliberately, but I do think that subconsciously we were trying to win support for what we were trying to do.

There are real consequences when we do this again and again and again. When we underperform, when we set up unrealistic expectations for ourselves and then fail to meet them, what we end up doing is deepening public cynicism about justice and government in general.

Lesson Three: Don't define success too narrowly. Reducing crime should be the central goal of the criminal justice system, no doubt, but this is not the only goal that matters.

I think that our default setting is to take a pass/fail approach to new programs. Did this work or not? Did it reduce crime or not? That's an important question to ask, but that's not the only question that matters. If we really want to build knowledge in the field, we have to be more subtle and nuanced and ask a more sophisticated set of questions about criminal justice reform.

[107] Paul Gary Wyckoff. *Policy and Evidence In A Partisan Age: The Great Disconnect.* Urban Institute Press, 2009, p. 3.

[108] Interview with David Wilson, "Trial & Error." http://www.courtinnovation.org/research/david-wilson-associate-professor-administration-justice-george-mason-university?url=research%2F16%2Fall&mode=16&type=all&page=1

Lesson Four: The line between success and failure can be blurry. It is not easy to separate the world into tidy piles of successes and failures. The truth of the matter is that there's a lot of gray out there. One example of this is the Harlem Community Justice Center, a program of ours that works with parolees returning to the neighborhood post-release from prison.

The Harlem Community Justice Center is located in the heart of East Harlem, at 121st Street and Lexington Avenue. As it happens, it is in the middle of a seven-block stretch that has one of the highest incarceration rates of any corridor in New York City, according to the Justice Mapping Center. Given this, we created a program that works with parolees coming back to the neighborhood and focuses intense supervision and services during the first six months after they are released. The explicit goal of the program is to reduce both crime and re-incarceration among participants. When our research team compared participants in the program to other parolees returning to Upper Manhattan who didn't go through the program, they found a 19-percent reduction in the reconviction rate. So it looks like the Justice Center has succeeded in reducing crime.

But when the researchers looked at technical violations, they found the program had almost doubled the number of people returning to prison for technical violations. This was largely due to a supervision effect. Because the Justice Center monitors participants closely, the program was detecting more dirty urines and missed appointments and broken curfews, which was leading to more revocations of parole.

We have tried to be scrupulous about disseminating the results of this study, both the bad and the good. I can tell you from first-hand experience that it is difficult to manage the message with something like this. The results of the Harlem study were truly mixed—some good, some bad. They're contradictory, and they're confusing and they require some effort to think about. Unfortunately, very few people have the time and energy to wade through these kinds of findings.

Lesson Five: Pay attention to politics. Some reformers tend to ignore politics. And some view politics as a negative force, the kind of thing that makes smart people do dumb things.

In reality, I think politics is pretty value-neutral. Politics can have positive impacts and politics can have negative impacts on criminal justice reform. A good example of this is the community court in San Francisco. The then-mayor of San Francisco, Gavin Newsom, came to New York a couple years ago and fell in love with the idea of a community court. And it really was Newsom's enthusiasm that jump-started this project. The project could not exist were it not for Newsom's support.

But because Newsom was a controversial figure, his relationship to the program also caused it enormous problems. Initially when the program came up for review by the board of supervisors in San Francisco, they voted it down. In my opinion, this vote had little to do with the merits of the project and everything to do with the board of supervisors' relationship to Newsom. The point here is that reformers ignore politics at their own peril.

Lesson Six: Context matters. There is basically no such thing as a program that can be taken off the shelf regardless of local conditions and implemented successfully.

We've seen this again and again: just because something works in one place doesn't mean it is going to work everywhere. An example of this is the drug court movement. I think there is a growing consensus that drug courts actually work, that they have been shown to reduce crime and substance. But that doesn't mean that every drug court is a success.

In *Trial & Error in Criminal Justice Reform*, we look at drug courts primarily through the prism of leadership. Leadership transitions are important moments for criminal justice programs. Many criminal justice reforms are created by highly charismatic individuals who inevitably go on to do other things. If we are serious about making criminal justice reforms stick, we need to be less reliant on heroic individuals. We need to spend more time building institutions that can sustain change over the long haul.

Lesson Seven: Things fall apart. Just because something works once doesn't mean it's going to work forever and ever. For example, Operation Ceasefire in Boston was a remarkable program. As David Kennedy has documented, Ceasefire was a collaboration involving local clergy, criminal justice agencies, street outreach workers, and academics from Harvard. Together, they accomplished some phenomenal results in the 1990s, including reducing youth homicides dramatically. Very, very few programs ever achieve success at the level that Ceasefire reached—the cover of *Newsweek* magazine, trips to the White House, millions of dollars in grants. In the midst of all this success, the program fell apart.

Why did it fall apart? There is an old cliché that failure is an orphan, but that success has many parents. This certainly seemed to be the case with Ceasefire. The great strength of this program was its interagency collaboration, but it was also the interagency collaboration that ended up killing the project. In the aftermath of the Boston Miracle, there were intense fights over who got credit for what. These fights ended up destroying the coalition.

When you buy a stock, they warn you that past performance does not guarantee future success. As the Ceasefire story indicates, this warning is true for the criminal justice system as well.

Lesson Eight: Reformers should invest in research. Self-examination is vital to the long-term health, not just of individual reform efforts, but of the entire field of criminal justice. We've seen this play out most recently in England with the community court in North Liverpool. The North Liverpool

Community Justice Centre has probably gotten more press attention than all of the other community courts in the world combined. It was actually the subject of a lightly fictionalized TV drama that aired on the BBC.

The North Liverpool Community Justice Centre was instigated really at the highest ranks of the British government. The home secretary at the time was personally involved in pushing the program forward. And, as often is the case when high-ranking officials get involved in something, there was enormous pressure to implement this project as soon as possible.

And in the rush to implement the Justice Centre, there simply wasn't time to build an effective information architecture for the project. A recent study of the Liverpool project concluded: "In practice, data collected is not routinely shared with center staff or in some cases appears not to be collected at all. This is not to say that the center isn't achieving significant outcomes, but that it is unable to demonstrate effectiveness." North Liverpool has basically found itself without adequate capacity to respond to critics who question both the efficacy and the cost of the project.

When times are tough, there is an enormous temptation to jettison "luxuries" like research and development. I think criminal justice officials should go in the other direction and deepen their investment in research because without research it is impossible to make policy arguments that are grounded in data. Without research it is impossible to rescue flagging initiatives if they start to fail. And without research it is impossible to prevent today's innovation from becoming tomorrow's conventional wisdom that needs to be overturned.

Lesson Nine: Failure is part of success. My friend Tim Murray from the Pretrial Justice Institute likes to say that no matter how much you poke it, twist it, or massage it, the criminal justice system has a remarkable ability to return to its original shape. I have no idea how to guarantee success in criminal justice reform, but the truth of the matter is that no one does. I do know how to guarantee failure, though, and that is to stop innovating, to stop testing new ideas.

What we should be doing as a field is encouraging criminal justice practitioners to fail again and again and again, so that they ultimately succeed.

10 Rethinking the Politics of Crime

This is a short op-ed that I wrote as part of the roll-out of Trial & Error in Criminal Justice Reform. It appeared online at the website of The Crime Report on August 10, 2010.

Not long ago, UK Prisons Minister Crispin Blunt gave a wide-ranging speech about criminal justice. Toward the end of his remarks, he devoted a single paragraph to arts programming in prisons, saying, "Arts activities can play a valuable role in helping offenders to address issues such as communication problems and low self-esteem." For the British tabloid press, Blunt's endorsement of arts programs for inmates was a gift sent from the slow-summer-news-day gods.

The front page of the *Daily Mail* heaped scorn on the announcement, declaring: "Now You Pay for Prison Parties: Tory Minister Says Taxpayer Must Fund Balls and Comedy Workshops for Criminals."[109] *The Mirror* summed up the same sentiment in fewer words: "You Clown."[110]

Moving quickly to halt the damage, 10 Downing Street distanced itself from Blunt. A spokesperson for Prime Minister David Cameron effectively drew a line under the matter, declaring, "We just want to make it clear to the public there will be no such parties."[111]

In all fairness, Blunt could have easily avoided the whole incident with a quieter approach to change. But while the "prison parties" controversy is of minor consequence and will no doubt soon be forgotten by everyone (save perhaps Crispin Blunt), it does offer a telling example of how an over-

---

[109]   Jack Doyle. "Now You Pay For Prison Parties: Tory Minister Says Taxpayer Must Fund Balls And Comedy Workshops For Criminals," *Daily Mail*, July 23, 2010.

[110]   Bob Roberts. "You Clown; No10 Tells Blunt: No Fancy Dress Fun In Jails," *The Mirror*, July 24, 2010.

[111]   "No 'Prison Parties' Says No10 After Blunt Comments," *BBC News*, July 23, 2010.

heated media and political culture complicates criminal justice policymaking. It's as true in the United States as it is in England.

It is fair to say that many American criminal justice officials live in fear of finding themselves in a similar position to Crispin Blunt: out on an island, on the wrong side of the "tough on crime" debate. This understandable fear has broad consequences for the field of criminal justice. Among other things, it creates a risk-averse environment where both policymakers and practitioners are reluctant to challenge the status quo and test new ideas.

This is a problem that Aubrey Fox and I examine in our book *Trial & Error in Criminal Justice Reform: Learning from Failure*. The central argument of the book is that criminal justice officials should adopt a lesson from the field of science, embracing the trial-and-error process and talking more honestly about how difficult it is to change the behavior of offenders and reduce chronic offending in crime-plagued urban neighborhoods.

In an effort to encourage greater reflection within the field of criminal justice, *Trial & Error in Criminal Justice Reform* tells the stories of several criminal justice programs that have experienced both success and failure, including drug courts, Operation Ceasefire and D.A.R.E. The trials and tribulations of these programs offer a host of important lessons, highlighting the challenges of inter-agency collaboration, the difficulties of managing leadership transitions and the gap that often exists between criminal justice researchers and practitioners.

Of all the obstacles that bedevil criminal justice reformers, none is more complex than mastering the politics of crime, particularly when the media gets involved.

In the United States, there are countless examples of cities and states passing "get tough" legislation quickly on the heels of horrific local tragedies that attracted frenzied media coverage.

These laws, which include truth in sentencing, mandatory minimums and three-strikes-and-you're-out legislation, often have unintended consequences. For example, California's efforts to reform its parole system and reduce the unnecessary use of incarceration have been hindered by an array of laws and ballot initiatives that have limited the flexibility and discretion of criminal justice officials.

Thankfully, some places have managed to avoid the fate of California. As we detail in our book, one such example comes from Connecticut, where state legislator Mike Lawlor found himself in the media spotlight in the aftermath of a horrible triple murder committed by two parolees who had been released from prison by the local parole board.

Local papers and elected officials clamored for someone to blame and something to do. Into this vaccum rushed advocates for three-strikes-and-you're-out legislation.[112]

Rather than fight this movement head on, Lawlor provided the media with another target: the failure of Connecticut's criminal justice infrastructure to communicate all of the necessary information about the parolees to the local parole board. By focusing attention on this mistake, Lawlor was able to use the media coverage to help pass nuts-and-bolts technology improvements rather than sweeping sentencing changes.

Of course, understanding the impact of media and political outrage is one thing; actually doing something about it is quite another.

For example, one criminal justice official in the United Kingdom recently acknowledged that even well-thought-out policy is often altered "at the slightest whiff of criticism from the popular press." He went on to promise a change from an era of policymaking with "a chequebook in one hand and the *Daily Mail* in the other."

The official? None other than Crispin Blunt.

---

[112] Luther Turmelle. "Triple Murder Fallout," *New Haven Register*, August 1, 2007.

PART IV

DEFINING SUCCESS

11 Small Sanities: A Look at the New York Miracle

*I have spent a fair amount of time in recent years in England work-
ing with criminal justice reformers both inside and outside of government. This work has led to the creation of the Centre for Justice
Innovation UK, a charitable organization dedicated to aiding local
innovators in England and Wales and creating connections with
leading American thinkers and practitioners. As part of the effort
to promote the Centre for Justice Innovation UK, which I sit on the
board of, I wrote this essay. It is an effort to bring a different perspective to the conversation about public safety in New York. It is not
meant to replace the usual narrative, which justifiably foregrounds
the work of the New York Police Department. Nor is it meant to be a
rigorous analysis of crime data. Rather, it is an attempt to offer an
addendum to the standard history, shining a light on some under-
reported facets of the criminal justice landscape in New York.*

The New York Story

In the years leading up to 1990, New York was a state with a reputation for
crime, drugs, and disorder. Much of this was driven—both in reality and in
public perception—by New York City, historically the source of six out of
ten criminal cases in a state of 20 million residents. No one seemed to know
how to stop the open air drug markets, street prostitution, and random
muggings, to say nothing of the violence: in 1990, there were 2,245 murders in New York City. Popular films of the day such as "Escape From New
York," "Taxi Driver," and "Warriors" depicted a city out of control, where
the law of the jungle prevailed. Nathan Glazer in *Commentary* magazine
spoke for many when he posed a fundamental question: "Is New York City
Ungovernable?"[113]

---

[113] Nathan Glazer. "Is New York City Ungovernable?" *Commentary Magazine*, September
1961.

What has taken place since 1990 is nothing short of remarkable. The murder total for New York City in 2012 was 417, a reduction of 81 percent since 1990. Indeed, since 1990, crime is down across the board in New York City: rape is down 53 percent; robbery down 79.9 percent; burglary down 84 percent; car theft down 94 percent.[114] Reviewing the statistics, Frank Zimring, author of *The City That Became Safe*, called it "the largest and longest sustained drop in street crime ever experienced by a big city in the developed world."[115]

These changes have been lost on no one who lives or works in New York. "Escape from New York" wasn't just a film: it was a fact of life. According to census data, from 1970 to 1990, the population of New York City fell by more than 572,000 as many residents with the resources to do so relocated to the suburbs and other safer locations.[116] As New York wrestled its public safety problems under control, however, the population flight reversed itself. From 1990 to 2010, the number of New York residents rose by more than 852,000. Public safety alone cannot account for these gains, but it has been a big part of the New York renaissance.

This story, and the role of the New York Police Department in making it happen, is fairly well known, if not well understood. Less well known is a crucial piece of the New York narrative: in addition to reducing crime, New York has also managed to reduce the use of incarceration.

From 1999 to 2009, the incidence of violent crime declined by 30 percent in New York State—it went down by only five percent in the rest of the country. At the same time, the prison population decreased by 18 percent in New York. In the rest of the U.S., the prison population increased by 18 percent during the same period.[117] In 1992, the average daily population in New York City's jail system was 21,000 inmates. By 2009, that number had dwindled to a little more than 13,000.[118]

As Frank Zimring has argued, what has happened in New York defies conventional thinking on both the right and left. After all, conservatives in the United States have traditionally argued that the key to crime control is stiffer penalties and increased incarceration. But New York has managed to get safer while locking up fewer people.

---

[114] CompStat. "Citywide," Volume 20, Number 26 (June 2013).

[115] Franklin Zimring. "How New York Beat Crime," *Scientific American*, July 28, 2011.

[116] New York City Department of Planning. "Population: 2000 Census Summary." http://www.nyc.gov/html/dcp/html/census/pop2000.shtml#citywide

[117] Michael Jacobson, "The High Cost of Prisons: Using Scarce Resources Wisely," *The Crime Report*, February 13, 2012.

[118] Sam Roberts, "As Crime Rate Drops, New York's Jail Population Falls to Lowest Level in 24 Years," *The New York Times*, June 11, 2010.

On the left, advocates have tended to argue that the key to crime reduction is addressing underlying social problems like economic inequality, discrimination, and family dysfunction. But there is little indication that any of these factors has fundamentally changed in New York City since 1990. With a few exceptions, the demographics of the City have remained basically static: New York City's economic indicators—unemployment, school drop-out, and poverty rates—have been and remain worse than the national average. If the conventional answers don't explain what happened in New York, what does?

The first thing to admit is that there is no definitive answer to how and why New York has been able to reduce both crime and incarceration. The truth of the matter is that cities are imperfect laboratories for social scientists. There are simply too many variables at work in a large urban setting like New York to be able to discern with any degree of precision what the active ingredients are. This essay is not an effort an effort to offer a definitive account of what is known in some quarters as "the New York Miracle." The innovative strategies pursued by the New York Police Department under Commissioner Raymond Kelly and other leaders have been well documented in other places—as has the controversy over the department's stop-and-frisk tactics. Instead, this essay highlights work outside of the police department, focusing on three areas: people, places, and process.

People

New York may have sent fewer people to jail and prison over the past 20 years, but this is not an indicator of decreased police activity. Indeed, there have been more police on the streets than ever before (peaking with 40,000 officers in 2000; there are now 34,500[119]) and officers have been more aggressive than ever, particularly with regard to minor offending. For example, from 2001 to 2010, misdemeanor arrests in New York City increased by 29 percent, from 194,496 to 251,169.[120]

So more cases are coming into the system, but fewer people are ending up incarcerated. Which raises an obvious question: what's happening to all of these people?

For many, the process of being arrested and arraigned—which typically takes 24 hours and includes time in a holding cell—is the sole punishment for committing a minor offense. This is an unpleasant enough experience to deter some from further offending.

But this is only part of the answer. Each year, thousands of New York-

---

[119] Michael Howard Saul. "Quinn Calls For More NYPD Officers," *The Wall Street Journal*, April 24, 2013.

[120] Gary M. Klass. *Just Plain Data Analysis: Finding, Presenting, and Interpreting Social Science Data*. Rowan & Littlefield Publishers, 2012, p. 106.

ers are linked to alternatives to incarceration, from short-term community service to long-term residential drug treatment. New York has long been blessed with an infrastructure of non-profit groups like the Vera Institute of Justice, Center for Community Alternatives, CASES, Osborne Association, Women's Prison Association, Fortune Society and others that are devoted to providing meaningful alternatives to incarceration and documenting their effectiveness. In recent years, this has been augmented by a network of specialized court-based programs, including drug courts, mental health courts and community courts, that offer judges meaningful community-based sanctions.[121] Importantly, many of these alternative-to-incarceration programs rely on judicial monitoring and the threat of jail time to promote accountability and ensure compliance.

As is typical of New York City, this patchwork of alternative programs has emerged organically without centralized planning. Some are funded by the City under the supervision of the Criminal Justice Coordinator's Office. Some are funded by the State. And some rely on federal funding or private donations. The field is constantly evolving as new problems emerge and new gaps in services are identified.

A particular area of focus at the moment is getting more sophisticated about using risk and needs assessments to allocate scarce resources where they are most needed. The latest research suggests that there needs to be a continuum of non-incarcerative interventions for offenders, with the most intensive options reserved for populations that are both high-risk and high-need.

"Risk" in this context refers to the personal traits that predict re-offending, including prior criminal history, anti-social personality disorder and anti-social peers. "Need" refers to problems like substance abuse, mental illness and a lack of job/life skills.[122]

In general, the higher an offender's risk level is, the more intensive his supervision should be. And the higher his need level, the more intensive the treatment. Indeed, there is evidence that linking low-risk/low-need individuals to intensive interventions such as residential drug treatment is not only a waste of resources but can actually be counter-productive, encouraging more criminal behavior. Thus the appeal of HOPE Probation, which places all participants in a drug-testing and monitoring protocol but reserves drug treatment for those who fail to succeed in the initial program.[123]

---

[121] The Center for Court Innovation has helped to pilot each of these models and to encourage their replication.

[122] For more, see Doug Marlowe. "Evidence-Based Sentencing for Drug Offenders: An Analysis of Prognostic Risks and Criminogenic Needs," 1 *Chapman Journal of Criminal Justice* (2009), pp. 167-201.

[123] Mark Kleiman. "Jail Break: How Smarter Parole and Probation Can Cut the Nation's Incarceration Rate," *Washington Monthly* (July-August 2009).

Given the prevalence of drug-related arrests, there is a natural temptation for those who are interested in reducing the use of incarceration to focus on the use of drug treatment as a criminal justice sanction. And while many addicted offenders do indeed need drug treatment, the truth is that there are many who do not meet the clinical diagnosis for addiction. For these offenders, drug treatment is not the right response.

Recognizing this, many frontline practitioners have begun to investigate the use of evidence-based interventions that target criminal thinking. For example, Thinking for a Change is a cognitive behavioral program that has been employed for many years in correctional settings. The idea behind the program is that by changing the way offenders think and respond/react to certain kinds of events, it is possible to change their behavior as well. Looking for opportunities to adapt the Thinking for a Change model to non-incarcerated populations—and to develop similar short-term interventions that would offer legally proportionate punishment for minor offenders—is a growing area of focus for many alternative-to-incarceration programs in New York.

Places

By and large, the criminal justice system tends to focus (however imperfectly) on people: police arrest suspects, prosecutors charge defendants, judges mete out sentences to offenders, etc. As necessary as this focus on individuals is, a big part of the New York success story has been about widening the lens of the criminal justice system to incorporate place as well as people.

This process began with the police and the embrace of Compstat in the early 1990s. Much has been written about the rise of Compstat, which is now used by dozens of police departments across the U.S. Starting under commissioner Bill Bratton, the New York Police Department made a substantial investment in technology and data analysis as a management tool to increase the accountability of local precinct commanders. One of the benefits of the Compstat approach was that it helped break down the city's crime problems into smaller, more manageable units of analysis; instead of a citywide phenomenon, police could focus on discrete precincts and individual neighborhoods with specific problems.

A natural companion to Compstat was the NYPD's commitment to "broken windows" policing (taking quality-of-life offending seriously as a way of promoting law and order and deterring more serious offenses) and "hot-spot" policing (increasing police presence on individual blocks, parks and other places with high crime rates). In *The City That Became Safe*, Frank Zimring credits "hot-spot" policing in particular with producing much of New York's public safety improvements.

Numerous studies have documented that crime is highly concentrated in certain locations. For example, Lawrence Sherman examined crime calls to the police in Minneapolis, Minnesota and found that about 3.5 percent of the addresses produced about 50 percent of the crime calls.[124] And criminologist David Weisburd has shown that, contrary to conventional wisdom, rooting out crime in a given location does not result in wholesale displacement; addressing an open-air drug market on one block does not mean that the criminal activity just moves around the corner. According to Weisburd, crime is a matter of the "convergence of suitable targets (e.g., victims), an absence of 'capable guardians' (e.g., police), and the presence of motivated or potential offenders."[125] Very few places have all three ingredients. Indeed, instead of displacement, Weisburd has found that areas adjacent to the sites that are the focus of intense police activity tend to experience crime prevention gains even though they were not the explicit target.

New York's focus on place is not confined to the operations of the NYPD. Since the early 1990s, this idea has spread to prosecutors (Brooklyn District Attorney Charles J. Hynes was an early advocate of community prosecution), defenders (Bronx Defenders has been a pioneer in community-based indigent defense), and courts (New York has a network of community courts that includes the Red Hook Community Justice Center in Brooklyn, which served as the inspiration for the North Liverpool Community Justice Centre).

New York's community courts in particular seek to bring many of the lessons from broken-windows and hot-spots policing to the judicial branch. Among other things, community courts have increased judicial attention to quality-of-life crime, helped criminal justice practitioners (not just judges, but attorneys and probation officers as well) gain a better understanding of the neighborhood context of crime, and targeted community restitution projects to clean up eye sores and hot spots identified by local residents.

Finally, it is important to note that the place-based work of criminal justice agencies in New York has been augmented by dozens of civic groups and business associations and community-based organizations that have devoted themselves to order maintenance and neighborhood beautification over the past generation. Taken together, these efforts sent a strong signal that disorder and lawlessness would not be tolerated on city streets. This in turn encouraged investment by both businesses and homeowners, creating a virtuous cycle with the appearance of order fueling improved public safety.[126]

---

[124] Lawrence W. Sherman. "Hot Spots of Crime and Criminal Careers of Places." *Crime and Place.* Crime Prevention Studies, Vol. 1 (1995), p. 36.

[125] David Weisburd, "Place-Based Policing," *The Police Foundation* No. 3 (January 2008), p. 4.

[126] George L. Kelling. "How New York Became Safe: The Full Story," *City Journal*, July 17, 2009.

Process

There is an increasing body of literature that documents the importance of informal social controls to reducing crime. While the criminal justice system tends to focus on formal mechanisms like the threat of apprehension and punishment, the reality is that most people obey the law because of their own internal moral compass and because of implicit and explicit pressure from their families, peers, and community.

David Kennedy, author of *Don't Shoot: One Man, A Street Fellowship and the End of Violence in Inner-City America*, neatly illustrates this point by asking audiences to raise their hands if they were afraid of the police as teens. Some people raise their hands, but most do not. He then asks listeners to raise their hands if they were scared of their mothers. Invariably, almost all hands are raised.

In places where informal social controls have been weakened, young people tend to see delinquent behavior as a sign of strength, incarceration as a rite of passage, and law enforcement as illegitimate. Adults tolerate disorder and are afraid to engage in public supervision of either the streets or local teens.

In recent years, various projects in New York City have sought to alter these kinds of conditions by revitalizing informal social controls and promoting voluntary adherence to the law. Tom Tyler, author of *Why People Obey the Law*, has suggested that if individuals feel that public authorities (police, judges, etc.) are legitimate, they are more likely to comply with the law. In a similar vein, if individuals feel that they have been dealt with respectfully—and are given an opportunity to voice their concerns—they are more likely to have faith in public institutions.

These ideas have been perhaps most powerfully embodied by New York's drug courts and community courts, which go to great lengths to involve local residents in the work of the courts and to communicate respect to litigants.

A recent study compared defendants in drug courts with those in traditional courts.[127] Drug court participants were one-third less likely to report drug use 18 months after admission to the program. And they were responsible for less than half as many criminal acts as the comparison group after 18 months.

The study showed that the strongest predictor of reduced future criminality was a defendant's attitude towards the judge. Having positive perceptions of the judge was also the greatest predictor of reduced drug use and reduced violations of supervision. This impact was seen across all demographics, regardless of race, gender, or criminal history. Even defendants

---

[127] Shelli Rossman, et al. "The Multi-Site Drug Court Evaluation," *Urban Institute* (November 2011).

with extensive prior involvement in the system or those who had received unfavorable sentences reported reduced criminality when they perceived the judge to have treated them fairly and respectfully.

The drug court study evaluated judicial interaction in two ways. First, researchers surveyed defendants about their perceptions of the judge. Defendants rated the judge on indicators such as approachability, respectful treatment, knowledge of the defendant's case, efforts to help the defendant succeed, and allowing the defendant to tell his/her side of the story. Second, researchers used structured court observations to document each judge's use of certain interactive behaviors, such as making regular eye contact, addressing the defendant directly and allowing him/her to ask questions, and providing explanations of court orders.

These same behaviors have also made a difference in New York's community courts. At the Red Hook Community Justice Center, nine out of ten criminal defendants reported that their case was handled fairly—a result that was consistent regardless of defendant background, charge, or case disposition. A door-to-door survey revealed that 94 percent of local residents rated the Justice Center favorably—a stark contrast to the 12 percent who rated local courts favorably before the Justice Center opened.[128]

In recent months, several New York City neighborhoods have sought to replicate some of these results by creating teen-led youth courts that train young people to hear actual low-level cases (truancy, graffiti, fare evasion, etc.) involving their peers. Youth courts rely on the idea of positive peer pressure. The young people who serve as attorneys, judges and jurors are essentially communicating to their peers that delinquent behavior is not acceptable. The youth courts recruit members based on their willingness to perform this role rather than their grade point average or their track record. (Indeed, those who have engaged in delinquent behavior in the past are encouraged to join as members.) Youth court participants receive intensive training and must pass a "bar exam" before joining the program.

Youth court sanctions are designed to be restorative rather than punitive: community service, letters of apology, and links to services. As valuable as they are in terms of training leaders and providing an early intervention for troubled teens, youth courts' most valuable contribution is probably symbolic: they are a potent symbol of the justice system being willing to cede a measure of authority to local voices and to engage in the co-production of justice.

Conclusion

In the end, it may or may not be possible to replicate the New York results in other places. As the singer Billy Bragg has written, "You can borrow ideas,

---

[128] Available at: http://www.courtinnovation.org/sites/default/files/RH_Fact_sheet.pdf

but you can't borrow situations."

As this essay has attempted to detail, dozens of different initiatives were at work simultaneously in New York over the past 20 or so years. Some of these initiatives were driven by policymakers at City Hall. Others emerged organically as individual agencies wrestled with the immediate problems in front of them.

One of the lessons of the New York experience is that the causes of crime are complex and there are no silver bullets when it comes to improving public safety. This point was made most eloquently by Adam Gopnik in a recent issue of *The New Yorker*:

> Epidemics seldom end with miracle cures. Most of the time in the history of medicine, the best way to end disease was to build a better sewer and get people to wash their hands. "Merely chipping away at the problem around the edges" is usually the very best thing to do with a problem; keep chipping away patiently and, eventually, you get to its heart. To read the literature on crime before it dropped is to see a kind of dystopian despair: we'd have to end poverty, or eradicate the ghettos, or declare war on the broken family, or the like, in order to end the crime wave. The truth is, a series of small actions and events ended up eliminating a problem that seemed to hang over everything. There was no miracle cure, just the intercession of a thousand small sanities.[129]

The American system of government is notoriously labyrinthine, with local, state, and federal agencies of overlapping jurisdictions and cross-cutting responsibilities. At its worst, this structure results in confusion, waste, and duplication of effort. At its best, it can create opportunities for innovation: there are multiple pathways for new ideas to bubble to the surface and find support.

Very few, if any, of the programs described in this paper originated among federal officials in Washington, D.C. This is not to say that policymakers in Washington played no role in the New York story. Among other things, Congress authorized funding to add police officers to the streets and to support the expansion of drug courts in New York and other states. And officials at the U.S. Department of Justice have supported intermediary organizations to provide training and technical assistance to would-be reformers on the ground level. Crucially, the federal government's investment in ideas like community court, community prosecution, and community policing has remained consistent no matter which party is in power.

This may be the ultimate lesson of the New York experience: the ability of local reformers to generate a "thousand small sanities" and the consistent willingness of national government to encourage and sustain them over the long haul.

---

[129] Adam Gopnik, "The Caging of America," *The New Yorker*, January 30, 2012.

12 Towards a More Rational and Reflective Justice System

In the summer of 2012, Professor Jane Donoghue invited me to participate in an international symposium on problem-solving courts held at the University of Oxford. These are my remarks from the conference.

I have spent more than 40 percent of my life working with problem-solving courts—the last ten years as the director of the Center for Court Innovation, a non-profit organization in New York that has been responsible for conceiving, implementing, and evaluating dozens of community courts, drug courts, mental health courts and other judicial reform efforts.

I have literally grown up as a professional alongside the field of problem-solving justice—in fact, the first drug court opened its doors in Miami, Florida the year that I graduated from college in 1989.

Over the years, I have seen many ups and downs as I have watched, and participated in, the development of problem-solving courts.

The negatives have included a handful of bad cases—cases where individuals who were released to the community by problem-solving courts used that freedom to do something harmful to themselves or to others.

The negatives have included searching critiques by scholars like Mae Quinn, James Nolan, and Eric Miller that have highlighted concerns about due process protections, net widening, and the appropriateness of attempting to solve individual and neighborhood problems in a court context. [130]

The negatives have included poorly-crafted evaluations that drastically overstated the impact of individual programs and helped to encourage

---

[130] See, for example, Mae Quinn. "The Modern Problem-Solving Court Movement: Domination of Discourse and Untold Stories of Criminal Justice Reform," 31 *Washington University Journal of Law and Policy* (2010), pp. 57-79; James L. Nolan. *Reinventing Justice: The American Drug Court Movement.* Princeton University Press, 2003; Eric J. Miller. "Embracing Addiction: Drug Courts and the False Promise of Judicial Interventionism," 65 *Ohio State Law Journal* (2004), p. 1479.

skepticism among researchers at a time when the field was just emerging.

And the negatives have included numerous examples of bad practice by problem-solving court judges and attorneys, including cases of *ex parte* communication, overly prescriptive court orders, and cringe-inducing lectures of defendants from the bench.

Balanced against these negatives have been a range of positives, of course.

The positives include a growing consensus among social scientists that drug courts have indeed proven effective at reducing substance abuse, recidivism, and government spending.[131]

The positives include the spread of problem-solving courts not only across the United States but internationally as well.

The positives include the fact that President Barack Obama has explicitly endorsed drug courts—and, in a time of fiscal restraint, the White House 2012 budget request sought $101 million for drug courts and other kinds of problem-solving courts.

But the biggest positive of them all has been the undeniable reality that thousands of lives have been improved by problem-solving courts—addicts who have gotten sober, mentally-ill individuals who have received the help they need, and families who have seen their parks cleaned and their streets made safer.

For me, the positives have far outweighed the negatives when it comes to problem-solving courts. The evidence suggests that, if implemented correctly, these projects are capable of making a positive impact—not only improving the lives of individual participants but the functioning and effectiveness of government systems as well.

Increasingly, researchers are asking not just whether problem-solving courts work but how they work and why. What are the ingredients that have enabled successful problem-solving courts to achieve positive results?

This is not a simple question to answer. Problem-solving courts are complicated enterprises, with lots of moving parts, including changes in judicial orientation, sentencing options, and monitoring protocols. Nonetheless, there are four elements that stand out as being crucial to the success of problem-solving courts: a commitment to changing the public conversation about crime, an emphasis on procedural justice and treating defendants with dignity and respect, a reliance on community-based alternatives to incarceration, and a capacity for, as well as a commitment to, self-reflection.

This essay examines each of these four (overlapping) elements, drawing from my personal experience as well as recent evaluations either performed by researchers at the Center for Court Innovation or using Center for Court Innovation projects as their subject matter.

---

[131] Shelli Rossman, et al. "The Multi-Site Drug Court Evaluation," *Urban Institute* (November 2011).

Changing the Conversation About Crime

My first exposure to problem-solving courts happened in the early 1990s, when I served as an intern during the planning of the Midtown Community Court, the first community court in the United States.

It is sometimes difficult to remember now, in the midst of what has been a sustained (and unprecedented) reduction in crime in many American cities, but public safety was in fact a dominant political concern in the U.S. in the early '90s. In fact, in the two presidential elections immediately preceding my introduction to the Midtown Community Court, crime-related moments were crucial turning points—first, the Willie Horton ad that undermined confidence in Michael Dukakis in 1988, and then the execution of Ricky Ray Rector that Bill Clinton used to prove that he was no bleeding-heart liberal in 1992.

As these examples suggest, the politics of crime in the U.S. in the 1980s and 1990s was dominated by get-tough rhetoric and a push to strengthen penalties for misbehavior. Many forces were at work here, including widespread public fear of urban crime and an increasing sense that it simply wasn't possible to rehabilitate offenders.

In 1974, sociologist Robert Martinson published an essay in *The Public Interest* about prison rehabilitation that came to be known by its depressing bottom-line conclusion: "nothing works."[132] According to Ted Gest, author of *Crime & Politics: Big Government's Erratic Campaign for Law and Order*:

> Martinson's conclusions merely confirmed what politicians and their constituents already believed. In policy terms, it provided ammunition to overhaul the laws on criminal sentencing in some states. The most popular idea was to mandate minimum prison sentences for specified offenses in order to prevent judges and wardens from setting convicts free after they had served only a few weeks or months. More broadly, the new sentencing structures ... narrowed the discretion of judges and corrections officials.[133]

This was the context out of which the first wave of problem-solving courts emerged in the U.S. It is fair to say that in making the case for reducing the use of incarceration and giving judges greater discretion in sentencing, the early advocates of drug courts and community courts and other such innovations were swimming against a powerful current.

For this reason, a great deal of care went into not only the design of the programs but the rhetoric that the early problem-solving courts used to de-

---

[132] Robert Martinson. "What Works? Questions and Answers About Prison Reform," *The Public Interest* 35 (1974).

[133] Ted Gest. *Crime & Politics: Big Government's Erratic Campaign for Law and Order*. Oxford University Press, 2001, pp. 198-199.

scribe their work. Many talked of "combining punishment and help" while "ensuring that all crime has consequences," and meeting "the need for swift and certain responses to misbehavior." In short, the initial problem-solving courts worked diligently to demonstrate that they were not in fact "soft on crime."

By and large, these efforts seem to have paid off. In the U.S., problem-solving courts are one of the few reform movements focused on reducing incarceration that has successfully appealed not only to those on the left of the political spectrum, but those on the right as well. For example, the conservative advocacy group Right on Crime, which is endorsed by a number of prominent Republicans including Newt Gingrich, Jeb Bush, and Grover Norquist, recently declared:

> In drug courts, America has found not only a solution to an important public policy problem, it has hit yet again upon an essential conservative truth—the power of personal responsibility and accountability.[134]

There are many reasons why Republicans have begun to embrace the idea of reducing incarceration (including the realization that correctional spending is an attractive target for government budget cutters), but the seeds for this remarkable development were planted nearly a generation ago by the first wave of problem-solving courts.

The Midtown Community Court was one such court. One of the explicit goals of the Midtown Community Court was to adapt some of the lessons of the broken windows theory to a court setting.[135] As articulated by George Kelling and James Wilson, the broken windows theory argued that minor offending must be taken seriously because it creates an environment that encourages more serious crime. In the 1990s, this idea was embraced by hundreds of police departments and prosecutors around the U.S., with the net effect of increasing state court caseloads dramatically over the course of the decade.

Midtown's approach proved to have broad political appeal. For conservatives, there was the focus on taking minor offending seriously and ensuring that those who committed offenses such as shoplifting, vandalism, and minor drug possession did not walk out of court without some sort of punishment. For liberals, there was the emphasis on alternatives to incarceration and links to meaningful social services. As a result, The Midtown Community Court was endorsed by the editorial boards of all of New York's

---

[134] "Priority Issues: Substance Abuse." 2010. http://www.rightoncrime.com/priority-issues/substance-abuse/

[135] Richard Curtis et al. *Dispensing Justice Locally: The Impact, Costs and Benefits of The Midtown Community Court*. Harwood Academic Publishers, 2000.

daily newspapers, from the conservative *New York Post*[136] to the liberal *New York Times*.[137]

Crucially, in seeking to improve the judicial response to low-level offending, the Midtown Community Court explicitly sought to increase the use of intermediate sanctions like community restitution and drug treatment. And, in fact, independent researchers from the National Center for State Courts found that the Midtown Court reduced the use of jail at arraignment by 50 percent.[138]

Over the years, the public conversation about crime in the U.S. has shifted. Today, there is widespread interest in rethinking the use of incarceration. By demonstrating that it is in fact possible to forge a response to criminal behavior that does not rely on jail as a default setting, the Midtown Community Court and other problem-solving courts have effectively helped to create space for a less punitive approach to justice in the U.S.

Treating Defendants with Dignity and Respect

In 2011, the Center for Court Innovation, the Urban Institute, and the Research Triangle Institute released the results of a multi-site study of drug courts in the U.S.[139]

The five-year study compared participants in 23 drug courts in seven different states to similar defendants who went through conventional case processing. Among other findings, the study documented that drug court participants were one-third less likely to report using drugs 18 months after their enrollment in the program. And they were responsible for less than half as many criminal acts as the comparison group after 18 months. Largely because of these reductions in criminal behavior, drug courts ended up saving an estimated $5,680 per participant.

In truth, these findings are hardly revolutionary. Indeed, the primary value of the study has been to underline the growing consensus among social scientists in the U.S. that drug courts are effective at reducing both substance abuse and criminal behavior.

---

[136] "...the proposed community court represents a creative effort to render a neighborhood plagued by petty crime both safer and more conducive to commerce." From "Community Crime, Community Justice," *The New York Post*, March 6, 1992.

[137] "Rather than impose fines or short jail terms ... the new court would sentence many [minor] offenders to useful tasks like cleaning graffiti, helping at soup kitchens or sorting trash at recycling centers." From "More Than Just a Court," *The New York Times*, July 17, 1992.

[138] For the four most common charges handled at Midtown, nine percent of defendants received jail sentences, compared to 18 percent of comparable downtown defendants. See Curtis et al. *Dispensing Justice Locally*, p. 2.

[139] Shelli Rossman, et al. "The Multi-Site Drug Court Evaluation," *Urban Institute* (November 2011).

But in addition to answering the bottom-line questions of impact and cost, the research team also decided to go a step further and look at the underlying reasons why drug courts were achieving positive results.

What they found was that the role of the judge is crucial. Put simply, when participants believe that they have been treated fairly and respectfully by the judge, they are more likely to succeed in treatment and remain law-abiding. Drug court participants had consistently more favorable perceptions of the judge than the comparison group. And the strongest predictor of reduced future criminality was defendant attitudes towards the judge. Having positive perceptions of the judge was also the greatest predictor of reduced drug use and reduced violations of supervision. This impact was consistent regardless of the race, gender, or criminal history of the defendant.

These findings offer strong support for the idea of procedural justice. As originally advanced by Yale Law professor Tom Tyler, procedural justice suggests that the perceived fairness of the court *process* is just as important, if not more important, than the perceived fairness of the court *outcome*.[140] Even those defendants who "lose" their cases rate the system favorably if they feel that the outcome was arrived at fairly. In his seminal book *Why People Obey the Law*, Tyler argues that procedural justice not only improves the satisfaction of individual litigants but actually improves compliance with court orders.

As a non-lawyer, I find the idea of procedural justice particularly compelling. One of my first experiences with the criminal justice system came in the early 1990s when I had a chance to sit on the bench with a judge in Manhattan criminal court for a week. It was an eye-opening experience, to say the least. I went in with a set of pre-conceived notions about how criminal courts in the U.S. operated, based largely on my reading of civics textbooks. Given New York's crime rate at the time, I expected to see a parade of major criminal cases. I also expected to see impassioned advocates and learned judges presiding over hard-fought trials.

My expectations, as anyone who has spent time in an urban American criminal courthouse can attest, were wildly off-base. The vast majority of the cases that I watched were not felonies but rather minor offenses—shoplifting, prostitution, minor drug possession and the like. There were no trials. And instead of fierce advocacy, what I saw were a lot of negotiated settlements as case after case was disposed of by plea bargain—often after only a few minutes of courtroom time.

But perhaps the most disillusioning part was just how difficult it was to follow what was going on. Everyone in the courtroom spoke in staccato bursts using legal jargon, acronyms and abbreviations. Nobody seemed to

---

[140] Tom R. Tyler. *Why People Obey the Law*. Princeton University Press, 2006.

make eye contact with anybody else. The only person in the courtroom who was consistently more befuddled than me was the defendant. Speed—the need to dispose of cases as quickly as possible in order to make room for the next defendant—was clearly a higher value than intelligibility.

I wish I could say that this situation is unique to New York, but in truth it is the prevailing reality in many American cities. This is why American courts are sometimes accused of dispensing assembly-line justice.

The best of the problem-solving courts push back against this trend. Along with their emphasis on individualized justice and regular judicial interaction with defendants has come a host of minor changes to standard courtroom communication techniques. This includes encouraging judges to make regular eye contact, to address defendants directly, and to provide explanations of court orders in plain English.

These seemingly modest modifications add up to something significant: an effort to restore the legitimacy of the justice system in the eyes of the public and, in particular, populations where distrust of government runs deep—the poor, minorities, immigrant groups, and others who find themselves disproportionately involved in criminal court. In performing this work, problem-solving courts are in sync with an emerging body of scholarly work by thinkers like David Kennedy, Tracey Meares, and Robert Sampson that highlights the importance of informal mechanisms of social control to creating and maintaining public safety.

By treating defendants with dignity and respect and communicating what happens in court more clearly not just to defendants but to the general public as well, American problem-solving courts are encouraging citizens (and non-citizens) to think of the justice system as fair, meaningful, and legitimate. This, in turn, promotes voluntary adherence to the law.

Promoting Alternatives to Incarceration

The most basic contribution that problem-solving courts have made to the field of criminal justice has been to alter sentencing practice in numerous courtrooms across the U.S.

Take for example, Bronx Community Solutions, a project that the Center for Court Innovation launched in 2005 in an effort to re-think how misdemeanor cases are handled in the Bronx, a borough of New York City that is home to roughly 1.4 million residents. Bronx Community Solutions serves as a conduit to community service and social service sanctions for dozens of judges in the centralized criminal court in the Bronx.

Over time, Bronx Community Solutions has indeed shifted sentencing patterns. In 2004, before the project opened, 15 percent of misdemeanor offenders in the Bronx received short-term jail sentences (less than 30 days) at arraignment. In 2008, following three years of Bronx Community Solutions, that figure had been reduced by 40 percent—only 9 percent of defendants received short-term jail sentences.

This change was accomplished by dramatically increasing the number of defendants who received alternative sanctions like community service or links to job training. In 2004, this happened in 9 percent of the cases in the Bronx. In 2008, the corresponding number was 25 percent. Each year, Bronx Community Solutions works with 11,000 criminal cases. If you do the math, Bronx Community Solutions is saving more than 18,000 days of jail each year in this way.

These numbers are not unique to Bronx Community Solutions. The Midtown Community Court has achieved similar reductions in the use of jail. And preliminary results from a forthcoming independent evaluation of the Red Hook Community Justice Center by the National Center for State Courts indicate that cases disposed at Red Hook were more likely than cases disposed in the conventional criminal court in Brooklyn to be sentenced to community service (33 percent v. 12 percent), to be sentenced to social services (27 percent v. 10 percent), or to be sentenced to a combination of both (18 percent v. zero). All told, 78 percent of the cases in Red Hook received a social service or community service sanction compared to 22 percent in the regular criminal court. According to the National Center for State Courts, Red Hook almost never sentenced defendants to jail at arraignment (1 percent of the cases), whereas judges in the conventional criminal court in Brooklyn sentenced 15 percent of their cases to jail.

There are a few caveats to offer here. First, not all problem-solving courts can claim that they produce less punitive outcomes than traditional courts. For example, many specialized courts dedicated to addressing domestic violence seek to strengthen penalties for batterers, including longer jail terms and increased monitoring of those in the community. And in some problem-solving courts, the price of avoiding jail or prison is often a criminal conviction, which can have long-term negative consequences for a defendant's employment and immigration status. (Although it also must be said that this practice is not unique to problem-solving courts and is, in fact, a standard part of plea-bargaining practice in conventional courts in the United States.)

Despite these caveats, the undeniable reality is that problem-solving courts have been a vehicle for offering a proportionate response to offending that does not simply default in mechanistic fashion to incarceration over and over again. The real-life impacts of this shift are enormous: literally thousands of individuals each year are being given an opportunity to avoid jail or prison and get their lives back in order. This is no small accomplishment.

Engaging in Self-Reflection

Few criminal justice innovations have ever been subjected to more scrutiny than drug courts. There have been literally dozens of experimental and quasi-experimental studies of individual drug courts by academic researchers. The investigative arm of Congress charged with auditing government programs (the Government Accountability Office or GAO) has performed two meta-analyses of drug courts.[141] An academic journal (*Drug Court Review*) is devoted exclusively to studying drug courts. And several national organizations are dedicated to identifying and disseminating best practices in drug court planning and implementation.

One of the by-products of all of this data and analysis has been the fostering of a sense of self-reflection among drug court practitioners. The capacity for self-analysis is not universal of course. There are many within the movement who are simply cheerleaders for the cause. And, in truth, every movement needs true believers who are willing to do the difficult work of arguing in the marketplace of ideas for more attention and more resources.

But alongside this strain of practitioner is a significant cadre of judges, attorneys, and clinicians who are committed to a process of continuous improvement, constantly looking at how drug courts are doing and attempting to enhance performance. For example, Doug Marlowe, a researcher at the National Drug Court Institute, has recently led an effort to examine how drug courts target participants.[142] He argues that rather than taking all comers or "creaming" first-time offenders, drug courts need to focus on a specific subset of addicted offenders—those who are both high-risk and high-need. Marlowe's analysis is already leading many drug courts to rethink their eligibility criteria and to get more sophisticated about their use of assessment instruments. This is an encouraging sign of the health of the drug court field as it matures.

Marlowe's effort may be the most important, but there are numerous examples of problem-solving courts engaging in self-analysis in an effort to improve their operations. Here are two case studies from projects operated by the Center for Court Innovation:

- At the Red Hook Community Justice Center, researchers noticed a spike in cases involving trespassing. It turned out that police were focusing their enforcement efforts on a particu-

---

[141]   U.S. Government Accountability Office's Report to Congressional Committees. "Adult Drug Courts: Evidence Indicates Recidivism Reductions and Mixed Results for Other Outcomes" (February 2005). Also, U.S. Government Accountability Office's Report to Congressional Committees. "Adult Drug Courts: Studies Show Courts Reduce Recidivism, But DOJ Could Enhance Future Performance Measure Revision Efforts" (December 2011).

[142]   Douglas B. Marlowe. "Targeting the Right Participants for Adult Drug Courts." National Drug Court Institute Vol. VII, No. 1. (February 2012).

lar building that was known locally as "the pharmacy" for the ready availability of illegal drugs. Based on this information, the Red Hook judge was able to make more informed decisions in these cases—and to communicate to defendants why that building was subject to special scrutiny. Additionally, the Justice Center was able to target the building for special community service projects.

- At the Harlem Community Justice Center, a community-based court in upper Manhattan, we operate a reentry court that provides parolees with enhanced services and supervision during the first six months of their parole term. The goal is to reduce both crime and incarceration. Researchers from the Center for Court Innovation tracked participants for three years and compared them to similar parolees who did not go through the program. They found that Harlem participants were 19 percent less likely to be re-convicted than the comparison group. Discouragingly, they also found that the increased supervision by a team of parole officers, social workers and an administrative law judge actually led to more Harlem participants going back to prison for technical violations of parole—missing an appointment, breaking curfew, flunking a drug test. Based on this evaluation, staff in Harlem have re-thought how the program responds to non-compliance, introducing a greater range of graduated sanctions, short of revocation, for rule-breakers.

At the Center for Court Innovation, we have made a particularly large investment in encouraging not only problem-solving courts but all criminal justice reform efforts to be more thoughtful and analytical about their own successes and failures.[143] We have made this investment because we believe that if the American justice system is ever going to live up to its highest ideals, it can't simply perpetuate the status quo. It must continue to improve, to test new ideas and to learn from its mistakes. At their best, problem-solving courts have embodied this process, providing a living, breathing example of a more rational and reflective justice system.

Conclusion

In the years since the first drug court was opened in Florida in 1989, problem-solving courts in the U.S. have had to confront a number of challenges. Would the first wave of drug courts and community courts and mental health courts be able to replicate their success in other locations? Was it

---

[143] These efforts are summarized in *Trial & Error in Criminal Justice Reform: Learning from Failure*, Urban Institute Press, 2010.

possible to survive changes in Presidential administration—from Democrat to Republican and back again—and the resulting shifts in federal criminal justice priorities? Would government funding for problem-solving courts at both the local and the national level be sustained even through economic downturns? And could problem-solving courts adapt to changing conditions on the ground and new research about what works best with offender populations?

So far, the answer to all of these questions has been a resounding "yes." But this begs a larger question: After a generation of effort, have problem-solving courts fundamentally changed the American criminal justice system? Here the verdict is less clear. Problem-solving courts still handle only a small fraction of the cases flowing through state courts. There remain many judges and lawyers committed to a more traditional approach to case processing. Notwithstanding the admirable efforts of people like David Wexler and others, many law schools educate their students much as they always have. And it is hard to argue that problem-solving courts have moved the needle nationally in terms of important indicators like the rate of incarceration or public confidence in justice or racial disparities.

The American justice system does not lend itself easily to quick fixes or silver bullet solutions. In the U.S., the administration of justice is a local, not a national, issue. To institute reforms means going state by state and, in many cases, county by county across a large, diverse nation. In this context, change will almost always feel piecemeal and take years to achieve.

Despite the claims of their most enthusiastic supporters, problem-solving courts are not a miracle cure for what ails our justice system. As a younger man, I might have found this disheartening. But as I have grown older, my time horizons have shifted. I no longer think that large, complex public institutions can be changed in two years or four years or even ten. Instead, I have come to understand and appreciate the importance of incremental progress. It may take a generation or more to achieve, but the values that problem-solving courts represent—a justice system that moves beyond simply being "tough on crime," that treats defendants with dignity and respect, that seeks out alternatives to incarceration wherever possible, and that is capable of self-reflection and self-correction—are worth fighting for no matter how long it takes.

Acknowledgments

This book would not be possible without the Center for Court Innovation, the institution that has been my professional home for the past 20 years. And the Center for Court Innovation would not be possible without the vision, leadership, and ongoing support of a number of important figures from the worlds of government and non-profit administration in New York, among them John Feinblatt, Mary McCormick, Judith S. Kaye, and Jonathan Lippman. I owe each of them an enormous debt for the trust they have placed in me to lead this remarkable institution.

Two decades is a long time to work in one place. I have managed to do so for two reasons: first, the Center for Court Innovation is constantly evolving, taking on new challenges and launching new initiatives. Just as important, the Center is full of remarkably decent and talented men and women. It is a pleasure to arrive at the office each day and get to work alongside professionals like Al Siegel, Adam Mansky, Valerie Raine, Amy Kotler, Liberty Aldrich, Julius Lang, Aubrey Fox, and Michael Rempel. I can't name every single person that works at the Center, but it is fair to say that this book would not exist were it not for the hundreds of people who work at our operating projects each day, attempting to change the lives of troubled individuals and make their local community just a little bit better. It has been my great fortune to chronicle this work.

One of the things that initially drew me to work for John Feinblatt, even before he founded the Center for Court Innovation, was his appreciation for the written word. I have tried to carry this value forward in the years that I have led the Center. Along the way, I have had the opportunity to collaborate with an array of co-authors who have helped sharpen my thinking and tighten my prose. Special thanks to: John Feinblatt, Aubrey Fox, Al Siegel, Adam Mansky, Phil Bowen, Derek Denckla, Robert Wolf, Emily Gold, Michael Rempel, Michele Sviridoff, Anne Gulick, and Carol Fisler.

Special thanks as well to Dylan Ruffi, who spent a long, hot summer helping me scrub the essays in this collection clean—finding citations, eliminating redundancy, and clarifying vague or imprecise language. This book includes both new material and work previously published in various magazines, journals, and websites. I have highlighted the original source material at the start of each chapter. I thank *Law & Policy*, *The Crime Report*, *Justice System Journal*, *Judicature*, and *American Criminal Law Review* for their permission to reuse and revise this work.

Speaking of permission, I thank my parents, Michele and Allan Berman, for giving me license to pursue my idiosyncratic ideas. Thanks as well to my brother M.J. and his family (Annie Lou, Charlie, Teddy, Scottie, Nell) and to the extended Vellenga family (Jim, Kathleen, Tom, Charlotte, Carlos, Julie, Stefan, Ian, Brendan, Aidan) for their support and encouragement.

Finally, the idea for this book came, as many of the best things in my life do, from a conversation with my wife, Carolyn Vellenga Berman. I thank her for simultaneously keeping me grounded and encouraging my imagination to take flight—no easy trick. I also thank my daughters, Hannah and Milly, for the joy and humor and inspiration they bring me on a daily basis, some of which I hope to have smuggled into these pages.

Permissions

Some of the chapters in this book are adapted from previous publications, and reprinted here with permission. Grateful acknowledgment is made to the original publishers.

"Justice in Red Hook" (with Aubrey Fox), *Justice System Journal*, Volume 26, No. 1 (2005).

"Learning from Failure," *Journal of Court Innovation*, Winter 2008.

"Problem-Solving Courts: A Brief Primer" (with John Feinblatt), *Law and Policy*, April 2001.

"Redefining Criminal Courts: Problem-Solving and the Meaning of Justice," *American Criminal Law Review*, Summer 2004.

"Rethinking the Politics of Crime," *The Crime Report*, August 1, 2010.

"What Is A Traditional Judge Anyway?" *Judicature*, October 2000.

Index

About the Author

Greg Berman is the director of the Center for Court Innovation, a public-private partnership located in New York City that seeks to reform the justice system through demonstration projects, original research, and technical assistance. Part of the founding team responsible for creating the organization, he has accepted numerous awards on the Center's behalf, including the Peter F. Drucker Award for Non-profit Innovation. Prior to being named director of the Center for Court Innovation, he served as the lead planner of the Red Hook Community Justice Center in Brooklyn.

Berman is the coauthor of *Trial & Error in Criminal Justice Reform: Learning from Failure* (Urban Institute Press, 2010) and *Good Courts: The Case for Problem-Solving Justice* (The New Press, 2005). In addition, his written work has appeared in *The Judges Journal* (guest editor), *New Statesman, The Guardian, Huffington Post, National Law Journal, Chronicle of Philanthropy*, and *Philadelphia Inquirer*, among other publications. He has served on numerous boards and task forces including: New York City Board of Correction, Wesleyan Center for Prison Education, Coro New York, Centre for Justice Innovation, Sloan Public Service Awards, Poets House, and the Police Foundation. He is a graduate of Wesleyan University and a former Coro Fellow in Public Affairs.

Visit us at *www.quidprobooks.com.*

CPSIA information can be obtained
at www.ICGtesting.com
Printed in the USA
LVOW04s1745021216
515533LV00009B/816/P